The Dogs of Nam

Stories from the Road & Lessons Learned Abroad

Christopher Kevin Oldfield

Cover design by Mitchell Arend
www.silentpartnerpictures.com

ISBN: 1985777304
ISBN-13: 978-1985777309

To the Road, in all her bitter glory.

And to my friends.
Take care, take care, take care.

ACKNOWLEDGMENTS

This book wouldn't have been possible if it wasn't for all the awesome, amazing, weird, and wonderful people I've met on the road. They have inspired me to keep exploring, to keep venturing out of my comfort zone. They have not only made me a better traveller, but a better person.

I also need to thank my family, who puts up with me being away for birthdays and weddings and funerals and everything in between. Thanks for always encouraging me to do whatever the fuck I want. You're all lovely.

Mad props are also owed to my cousin Mitch, who rocked the design for this little book. He and I have had some adventures of our own, with more to follow in the future, I hope! I also need to thank all my friends who helped with the first round of editing. They were my guinea pigs, and I can't thank them enough.

And last but certainly not least, I need to thank my partner, Christine. Not only does she tolerate my incessant wandering but she puts up with me dragging her around the globe on haphazard quests for adventure. She's a good sport (most of the time) and I love her to bits.

Prologue

I remember the first time I died. It happened in Costa Rica, on a mountain, lounging in the crown of a tree I had just inelegantly scrambled up. I was in the clouds, miles from civilization and a lifetime away from home. The rain had shed her weight, more mist, now, than anything else. It was in your lungs, on your tongue; a floating ocean in the sky. I died right there, in the canopy. Sideswiped and crushed, bleeding out to a perfect moment.

I've died a million times since. On crowded trains and down sketchy alleys, in cramped dorm rooms and on broken squat toilets half a world away. I've watched my ashes scatter, seeds to feed the chaos, heart and arteries mere fuel to the atlas fire.

And you? Where are you in all this?

Maybe you're out here bleeding with me, leaving piss stains and blood trails and swelling hearts across the globe. I hope you're out here, wandering and connecting, caution long since thrown to the wind. If that's the case, you'll be familiar with the stories that follow, and the awkward, chaotic mess that the Road offers up. For you, this book will be a kick of strobe light nostalgia, a reminder that the world is a beautiful mess worth exploring.

For those of you dreamers who aren't with us, stuck behind a desk, imprisoned by a lifetime of responsible choices…well, I hope this book is a slap in the face. A wake-up call. Because we need you out here with us. Whether it's for a day or a week or a month, we need you. You need you.

So pack a bag, leave your inhibitions and expectations at the gate, and come and learn some lessons the hard way.

We're waiting for you.

This Is Not the Best Travel Writing

A Lesson in First Impressions

They say the best travel writing must have an angle. There must be a narrative, an arc of some kind. The writer must investigate some peculiarity of his location or set out on a quest to discover something new — or rediscover something old. There must be a beginning, a middle, and an end. There must be a *point*. Without an angle, travel writing devolves into mere anecdote, falling from its lofty and respected heights into the crude and uncouth realm of *storytelling*. Now, I was never one for lofty anything so it should stand as no coincidence that what follows is hardly the best travel writing.

Travel writing, as enlightening as it can be, tends to impose a narrative where there may not be one, as if life was somehow coaxed into following a script. If that's what you are in search of then please put this book down and look somewhere else. Those stories, the kind that win awards and are found, piecemeal, in collectable anthologies, are fabrications, illusions. They involve interviews and research, pitches and pegs. They are much like theatre in that we only see what is presented, yet what is presented could never have come to pass without the shadowy actions of those backstage. The best travel writing often involves forced experiences, a greasing of the palms of serendipity. Of course, great travel writing — much like great theatre — is entertaining and informative. And yes, it often does involve serendipitous events but serendipity is not the backbone of great travel writing. People make a living writing travel stories, and I dare say you can't rely on serendipity for your income.

In addition to not being the best travel writing, this book is also not a *"How To"* for budget travel. It won't tell you how to travel the world for cheap. It won't tell you how to get a visa extension in Thailand or how to plan a Trans-Siberian trip across the Russian steppe. It won't delve into the mysterious world of travel hacking or how to prevent bedbugs if you find yourself in some dingy hostel in a backwater town in South East Asia. The world is full of books and blogs with all that information and more — including my own. Besides, you're already smart enough to figure out that shit out on your own.

What is this book, then? It's a collection of stories, plain and simple. What kernels of fortune cookie wisdom you glean from them is on you. For me, these stories, and the lessons I have extracted from them, represent the essence of travelling...as if words could somehow capture the sacred act of *going somewhere new.* This is a collection of tales and reflections, genuine and unfiltered. These stories have become woven into the fabric of who I am, who I have become over a decade of wandering and exploring this pretty blue planet that we live on. They serve (or so I hope) as illuminating snapshots into the glamorous world of budget backpacking, a realm of sharing and learning and growing. All too often travel is reduced to the superficial. It is spit deep and bland, an exercise in calloused hashtag vanity. For me, these stories are reminders that travel can be stubborn and wild and untamed. It can be your heart overrun, thin-skinned and gaping.

These stories paint an honest picture of what lies beyond the stifling routines of modern day life — for better or worse. This is what travel looks like beyond the unrealistic filters of Instagram, beyond the curated photo albums of Facebook. These stories — like travel itself — involve connections, realizations. They dredge up hidden feelings, uncovering new-found perspectives just when you least expect it. They explore the fine art of looking into the mirror and seeing the universe unfold before you, in all its beauty and horror. At its core, this book is about letting go and being swept away into the tidal chaos of being.

Welcome, friends, to my lessons learned abroad.

Christopher Kevin Oldfield

in a city of stray dogs
caught and killed
we wander
like the dogs of nam before us
we spend our final days
unknowing

Christopher Kevin Oldfield

Falling in Love with Chaos

A Lesson in Serendipity, Seatbelts, and Stalkings

My first trip beyond the borders of Canada was to Florida. The year was 1995, and I was going to Disney World. One week at Disney was about as awesome of a trip as a 10-year-old could wish for, and as soon as I found out my old man and I were going I started saving my money. At 10, I wasn't really bringing in the big bucks but I did what I could to make sure my piggy bank stayed brimming. I scraped up every bit of loose change that found its way between the couch cushions and every dollar from the tooth fairy was tallied and added to my hoard. Each penny I passed on the street was diligently collected, and the few bucks I made doing chores were saved. Come our departure I had a few hundred dollars to blow at the most Magical Place on Earth.[1]

What stands out in my mind now, some twenty years later, isn't any of the main attractions from that trip. It isn't the sudden plunge of Splash Mountain or the sickening spins of that stupid teacup ride. It isn't even the delicious (and overpriced) beer nuts you could buy every twenty paces at Typhoon Lagoon or Blizzard Beach. And no, it isn't even the JAWS ride, though that shit was both epic and terrifying. The part of that trip that stands out in my mind the most, the memory that is both vivid and profound, is the automatic seatbelt in our rental car.

Seriously.

Sure, spending quality time with my dad was great, and it's something I'll cherish until the end of my days...but those seat belts! Our car was a Saturn, a company that doesn't exist anymore, no doubt because those seatbelt contraptions were terribly impractical. You see, our car had a seatbelt that *automatically* slid up and down whenever I entered the vehicle. Open the door, and the little motor buzzed to life, chugging along a track to allow me to sit down. Close the door, and it would reverse and lock me safely into my chair. I was in awe, truly, every time I entered the vehicle. The future was happening, then and there, and it was mesmerizing. Outside of the ten-minute drive to and from Disney World an automatic seatbelt was probably an unwieldy contraption, but for 10-year-old me it was the most incredible thing. God Bless America, etc.

Looking back, I think that story sums up the reason why I — and many other people — travel. More often than not, the best things we discover are rarely what we plan and almost never what we expect. I'm sure that very reason keeps a lot of people from traveling, for who wants unexpected headaches and the insecurity of serendipity when they can have the tyrannical comfort and pseudo-security of a well-oiled, modern day routine? Don't get me wrong, I love it when things go smoothly; when a plan is seamlessly executed without a hitch it is an amazing feeling. But over the years I've learned to fall in love with chaos. Because that's what life is: a big, chaotic mess chock full of weird and fun and terrible experiences that mould and shape us in more ways than we can ever comprehend. Being alive is a ridiculous exercise, plain and simple. There really is no rhyme or reason to it, and that visceral ridiculousness is forever amplified on the road. Travelling, backpacking, vagabonding, *whatevering* — it's there where you will discover the best and the worst that humanity has to offer. You will see beauty and tragedy, poverty and affluence all ebbing and flowing as you wander this wide world of ours. Most of that stuff you will never even see coming. No matter how much you plan, how much you prepare, you will inevitably encounter situations that drop an emotional roundhouse straight to the feels. I suppose that's why I still travel: I have come to love and appreciate the value of being blindsided by the overwhelmingness of being alive. Call me old fashioned.

That appreciation of the unknown eventually blossomed, prodding me to take my first "real" trip outside of Canada.

I had just finished my inaugural year of university and found myself craving a change of scenery. Sure, my classes were enjoyable and I had made some great friends...but something was missing. Every day I woke up and hit the gym, attended all my classes (ok, I skipped 3 classes that year), and handed all my assignments in on time. I worked a full-time job, as well, often waking up at 4am to diligently stock the produce shelves at a local grocery store. In short, I was rocking a hyper-efficient but mundane routine. I needed a break. I needed new sights and sounds and smells, a reprieve from the workaday world that I was engrossed in. I needed a holiday, but more than just a holiday, I needed some fresh air.

During the dark and bitter months of the Canadian winter I began researching my options — what to do, where to go, how much I could afford to spend. It all ended up being for nothing, however, for one day on campus I found a flyer for a small company leading students to Costa Rica. The trip was even eligible for course credit, and so I decided to check it out. Two weeks later I had myself a ticket to Costa Rica. My program wasn't eligible for course credit, but that didn't bother me — I was about to head to Central America!

After a short layover in New Jersey, that is. Ugh.

For two weeks, I hung out off the grid in the jungle learning about sustainable living. For someone who had spent a few years working on an organic farm it was exactly as amazing as I had hoped. I shared potato-planting hacks with the residents and brushed up on my composting knowledge. I went for jogs in the rain and did yoga every morning on a cliffside plateau. It was paradise, silent and beautiful. It was also terrifying.

The very first anecdote our guide told us when we arrived was a story to impress upon us the dangers of our new environment. It was not a happy story.

Years ago, when our guide was a teenager he and his friend would play in the forest. Personally, I didn't really consider the jungle to be a "kid friendly" environment but what did I know. Apparently, it's pretty standard for kids in Central and South America to cut loose in the rain forest. Sure, I played in a forest when I was a kid, too, but my forest was a lot less *kill-y* than his.[2]

Now, this best friend of his was really interested in birds. During his rainforest romps, he would spend his free time bird watching. One day, he was hiking along a trail when he heard some baby birds. He followed the noise to a hidden nest, recognizing the type of bird by their little baby bird noises. He figured the birds were crying because they were hungry, and so he reached in to pull one out, just to take a look. Curiosity, alas, does in fact kill.

The birds were not screaming because they were hungry, but rather they were screaming because they were being eaten by a snake. When the boy reached in, the snake lashed out in surprise, biting his hand and pumping his veins full of venom. Naturally, the boy panicked.

He started to run back to his village, which a few kilometers away. The exertion sped up the poison and he ended up dying alone on the trail.

Welcome to Costa Rica.

Our chipper guide didn't stop there, however. He followed the anecdote up with an important public service announcement: check your boots and shoes before putting them on your feet. Footwear, we learned, makes cozy quarters for snakes and spiders and God knows what else. Each day we were reminded to shake out our footwear in the off chance something had moved in. Fortunately, mine remained empty for the duration of my trip. Probably because of the smell.

After our uplifting introduction, we were shown to our cabins. Built into the mountainside, they were rustic and charming wooden huts, each built by the residents that lived there with materials that were carried — by hand — to the location. While far from luxurious, the cabin-huts were certainly a cut above what one might expect in the middle of a jungle on a mountain. Our huts even had minimal electricity, powered by a small wind turbine and a nearby DIY hydro project. Hot water, however, was non-existent. You want delicious, ice-cold, fresh mountain water? They've got aplenty, and it was the best water I had ever tasted. But it was the absolute worst for showering. You can light me on fire and I won't bat an eye, but toss a few cold drops of water on my skin and I'll shriek like a banshee. Being cold is my Kryptonite, which makes me the saddest excuse for a stereotypical Canadian there is.

After a day of crushing and aerating compost, I made an attempt to rinse away the fragrant odours that clung to me in the humid jungle. I didn't last more than 12 seconds under the pressurized onslaught of that icy death water. I gave up showering then and there. For the next 11 days, I remained o'natural. Here's to conserving water.

I shared my hermetic forest hut with another Canadian whose name I have long forgotten, but who nevertheless left an impression almost as lasting as those automatic seat belts. You see, this guy — let's call him Bert — was really into Devil Sticks.

For those of you who don't know, Devil Sticks were a 90's fad, much like the Yo-Yo, Jacks, Pogs, Crazy Bones, Pokémon, and lots of other crap you can look up if you are curious. As with all fads, eventually everyone dropped Devil Sticks and moved onto whatever quirky activity came next. Except Bert. He stuck with those Devil Sticks...for, like, another decade. Hell, he was so into them that he even made his own out of repurposed tire rubber. He could toss and throw those sticks something fierce. One handed, behind his back, upside down — he could do it all. For a slightly out of shape, generic-looking student from northern Ontario he was incredibly dexterous.

Having never dabbled much with Devil Sticks, myself, I figured it was perhaps time I gave them a whirl. As an occasional player of the drums, I considered myself at least slightly above average when it came to hand-eye coordination...but Bert had me beat by a mile. I could keep it up for a few seconds (heyyy-ohhh) but Bert was by far the king of the D-Sticks. Twenty bucks says he still gives 'em a toss to this day, and good on him.

For our last two days in the jungle, Bert, myself, and the rest of those visiting the biological reserve went for an overnight hike to the summit of our mountain. We were in the foothills of the Cordillera de Talamanca, a mountain range that extends along Costa Rica and down into Panama. The plan was to hike to the summit, camp out, and hike back down the next day. Easy peasy. It was a six-hour trek up the mountain, and even today I still find it hard to describe. Breathtaking vistas of rain and cloud forests, beautiful flora, rolling fog; even in the torrential downpour it was an unforgettable sight. It wasn't long before mud covered most of our extremities as portions of the climb were more scramble than hike. The warm rains slowed our progress as the narrow trail turned to mush under our climb, but we were by no means in a rush. We stopped to admire every flower within reach, their smells foreign and refreshing; their names irrelevant; their beauty unremitting. You could feel the thickness of life in the air, taste the very exhalations of the earth.

Beauty, however, came at a cost.

We were not far up the trail when the first surprise found me. As I looked up to find my footing I saw that the woman in front of me, a quick-paced bubbly blonde, had a spider on her bag. Thinking nothing of it, I mentioned it to her. She froze. Her eyes were wide as she stood motionless, petrified, as sweat and rain trickled down her flushed face. She was not, I gathered, a fan of spiders. I nonchalantly reached over and flicked the little gaffer aside and watched it scurry away. It was only then that I realized it wasn't just some run-of-the-mill spider.

It was a baby tarantula.

The reality of my location truly seeped in after that. I suppose I'm just lucky it wasn't something worse.

As we worked our way higher, the journey became arduous. The steep angle of ascent gave each of us difficulty in the on-again, off-again rain. As we crossed over a wind-swept clearing and back into the jungle I reached out to grab a tree to use as an anchor to haul myself up. I was immediately seized by our guide. Protruding from the tree were hundreds of small spikes, sharp thorns I hadn't noticed as I reached for it. How my hand had not been punctured was a miracle, for those concealed spears jabbed through every gap between my fingers. Our guide quipped that if I were to have been stabbed I'd need to visit the hospital immediately...*emergency evac* immediately. Whether he was telling the truth or joking just to scare me, I was not quite sure. Suffice it to say, I didn't push my luck. I made sure to keep my hands away from all the trees — not an easy task in a rain forest.

Crises averted, we trudged onward through the brush over mud-slicked trails. Nothing was waterproof in that weather (my poncho didn't even survive the first few hundred meters of jungle). It didn't matter, though. The air was so fresh, so crisp, it felt weightless in my chest; we were breathing air straight from the lungs of the world, filling ourselves with its purity and simplicity as warm rain washed away everything but the moment. We carried on, exhausted yet reborn in the clarity of our task and beauty of our surroundings.

We climbed higher still, rising above the clouds. Eventually we were left peeking over the cliff edges to stare down at the rain *below* us. Like the Gods of Old, we towered above the world. Our domain stretched for miles in the lush haze. It was one of those jaw-dropping, awe-inspiring events that would have made a great photo, the kind someone would slap a generic feel-good quote to and toss up on Instagram, or maybe even post as their Facebook cover photo.

Yeah, it was that great.

I knew then and there that I had to travel again. The world was too beautiful not to explore.

I must admit, however, that I was a bit concerned before I left for Costa Rica. I had allergies to pollen, dust, hay, cats, and probably a bunch of other crap out there in the natural world. The Great Outdoors were an ironic nemesis to my immune system and so I stocked up on allergy meds in anticipation of itchy eyes and a stuffed-up nose. Miraculously, I found that I wasn't much bothered during my two weeks in the rainforest, for some reason no doubt easily explained by science. With that in mind I didn't bother to pack them for our final trek up the mountain. Amusingly/Ridiculously, this may have saved my life.

As we neared the summit my eyes became itchy and my nose starting to run...but I didn't care. I was literally on top of a MOUNTAIN, gazing out over a vast and biodiverse panorama brimming with life. We clambered up some trees to lounge and rest, letting our senses explore our new environment. To the east, we could just barely make out the shape of the Atlantic Ocean, straining our eyes through the foggy mist. To the west, the Pacific lay also within sight, though partly obscured by the ever-changing weather. We stayed in those trees for some time, digesting the indescribable sights as deeply as we could. We were tattooing the view on our soul, stitching it to our marrow. We were reborn, there, cradled by the mountain, a second wind dancing in our gut.

Eventually, though, it had to end.

I climbed down from my perch and called everyone to a makeshift clearing so we could take a group picture. Preoccupied with the incredible view, nobody came. I stood there waiting with my disposable camera like a chump, resisting the urge to rub my now-burning eyes, a side-effect from my allergies. It was just myself and one other traveller who were assembled and waiting for the photo op. She was maybe 5'2" and weighed in at a fragile 90lbs or so. Obviously, she was tougher than she looked because she had made it to the peak with the rest of us. The two of us stood there awkwardly, waiting for the group to meander toward us, though they all seemed quite content to continue with their treetop R&R. So, we waited. And waited. And my allergies got worse, my eyes burning from the inside-out. And that's when I smelled something, a familiar something you don't want to smell when you're alone in a jungle.

I smelled a wet cat.

It suddenly clicked. Allergies — cat allergies, to be specific — were the cause of my irritating condition. I had enough time after the thought registered to turn around, reaching out to grab my impatient co-hiker. It was then that I heard something, deep and low. A soft growl came from the trees nearby, slowly circling toward us. It wasn't loud, just audible enough if you listened closely. It sounded exactly like the purr of a cat as it sleeps, but decidedly more frightening. It was, I discovered, a jaguar. And it was only 12 feet away.

I heard it moving in the brush and tracked its direction by the low rumble of its growl, catching glimpses of movement here and there as it edged in closer. I stood in front of my companion and pulled out the only weapon I had: a Swiss Army knife. Armed with a 2" blade I knew this would not end well. Sometimes, friends, size does matter.

We held our ground as it circled closer, the intensity of the moment skyrocketing in my chest. Surprisingly, I was not as scared as I should have been, considering that my demise was imminent. I suppose when there is no hope of escape there really isn't much to fear. In truth, I only had to outrun my petite companion, but knowing my luck, she (like Bert) no doubt had some sort of hidden talent that would leave me left for dead. So, I held my ground, mediocre blade extended to meet my feline fate head on. If I was going down, I was at least giving the beast a bothersome flesh wound.

Branches suddenly snapped and cracked behind us, sending me to jolt in surprise. The group was finally coming down the slope and the clatter was just enough to cause the cat to pause and my heart to lodge itself in my throat. I immediately motioned for the group to stop, gesturing with my hands to get their attention. Our guide could tell there was a problem; I guess the colour draining from my face was something of a clue. He reached into his bag and kept his hand there, clutching the loaded pistol he occasionally used to defend himself from ever-encroaching poachers. I did my best to convey the situation to him by means of a creative gesture.

I pointed to the bushes nearby, stabbing my finger toward the cat. I tried to make a scary face to illustrate what lay hidden within pouncing distance. I bared my teeth, raised my hands into mock claws, and then pointed once again to the vicinity of the hunter. I must have looked like a complete and utter idiot, BUT, the gesture got my point across. So, whatever. It seemed reasonable at the time.

We all stood as still as possible, statues in the quiet jungle. Our guide paused as well, waiting to see what would happen next. No movement. No sound. Just an unnatural stillness in a jungle full of life. Our guide cautiously made his way down toward me and the group followed his brave lead. The noise of them all clambering down the slope seemed to have kept the cat at bay, deterring its attempt at a quick — but scrawny — meal. We waited a little longer to make sure the coast was clear before trekking onward and downward. For whatever reason, I lingered at the back of the pack as everyone passed, just to see if the kitty cat was still around. It was. It followed us for a few hundred feet before disappearing back into the misty forest.

Chris 1, Jungle 0.

For what it's worth, I now travel with a larger knife. Lesson learned.

~~~~~

The icing on the cake for this trip came a few days later when we were kayaking in the Pacific Ocean. Our little beach hut was situated perfectly at the crest of a wide bay skirted by mangroves. It was the scene of a constant battle between the ocean and the river, the waves kicking up a heck of a ruckus as they capped and crashed, salt water meeting fresh. To access the beach, we had guided our boat through watery war zone with a reckless abandon, holding on tight for dear life as we ploughed through the perpetual chop. We were warned to be extra careful there, for many a boat had capsized in the tumultuous stretch of water. For that very reason, it was now a shark-infested section of the bay. I cannot describe the whiteness of my knuckles as I clung to that boat. Now, maybe the warning was a little more "guide humour" to keep us ignorant tourists on our toes. Maybe it wasn't. Either way, when we got out into our kayaks a few hours later we made sure to steer clear of that area...and I made sure never to paddle too far away from the group.

Eventually, some of us decided to head up a river channel in a foolish attempt to battle the rapids in our sea kayaks and test our manly selves against the current. I don't recall who made it the furthest up river, but I'd wager it wasn't me and it likely wasn't far. On our way back, exhausted from the fruitless competition, we saw a bunch of crocodiles (or alligators, I can never remember how to tell the difference) chilling out in the sun. Just like on the Discovery Channel, these bad boys were motionless, perhaps dozing off in the 40-degree heat. Motionless, that is, until they weren't.

Glancing back, one of those lazy fuckers was already halfway into the water and heading our way. Its thick tail waved and slipped into the dark water, disappearing under the surface. Nothing but a few ripples were visible, and they were rippling our way. Somebody cursed (probably me) and we paddled like fiends to get out of there. We all were yelling, our arms pumping furiously toward the ocean. We didn't bother to look back. We just paddled for dear life.

It was all over within 30 seconds and fortunately it didn't end with a waterlogged corpse bobbing downstream. The beast had given up and swam back ashore, letting us catch our collective breathes as we laughed like mad men in our tiny, plastic sea vessels.

Chris 2, Jungle 0. Icing on the cake, indeed.

~~~~~

I got lucky with this trip. First off, I wasn't maimed or killed which is always plus. I was able to meet some incredibly kind people, get a little first-hand experience of a culture and country vastly different from where I was from, AND I picked up a few stories that I can toss out when I meet new people and need to sound cooler than I actually am. Overall, like my trip to Disney World, Costa Rica was a serendipitous success. Naturally, it made me want to travel more. I wish I could say solely to meet great people and see wonderful things, but honestly, I love to travel for the stories. Like many writers, I love to spin a good yarn for an eager listener, to share vivid portraits of life beyond the familiar. But infinitely more than that I love *living* those stories. Few things are more addictive than both routine and adventure...and it was clear I had had my fill of routine.

Christopher Kevin Oldfield

A Vegan in Mongolia

A Lesson in Being Polite

When I was a kid, I used to catch tadpoles. They swam around in a muddy pond near my house and we would scoop them up in old margarine containers. After we snagged a handful we would carry them back to the neighbourhood. There, at the side of my friend's front lawn, was a big electrical box. It was shiny and green and sizzled in the summer heat, always hot to the touch. This was where we did our research.

Spooning out the tadpoles, we would pour them onto the electrical box and watch them cook. The droplets of water would bounce and evaporate, the tadpoles doing the same. Their burnt little bodies would stick to the scalding green paint, leaving faded black markings as they shrivelled to smoke and dust before our very eyes. We watched the entire process, transfixed on our callous experiment.

That was my first real experience with death, with standing witness to the irreversible transition. Less than a decade after those experiments, I gave up eating meat — and anything else that came from animals. I had been working on a farm, and I couldn't bring myself to kill the animals I had spent the season raising. I had come to see that they were intelligent and unique and deserving of a decent life. When I looked at them I saw my humanity reflected back at me, fragile and fleeting. I couldn't bring myself to kill them, and it seemed only fair that if I couldn't kill them, I shouldn't ask others to do it in my place.

So, I went vegan. That was almost 15 years ago. I can't help but wonder the part those tadpoles played in my decision.

I never found transition that challenging as North America has plenty of food options available for every sort of lifestyle (though I confess I wasn't always the healthiest vegan). It wasn't until I was a million miles from home in a country I never thought I'd step foot in that my first real challenge came...

~~~~~

Mongolia. Hardly a culinary paradise for vegans. In hindsight, that seems an embarrassingly obvious fact, but you know what they say about hindsight. Being a desert nation where nothing really "grows" (Only 1% of the country's arable land is used for crops), the fact that there isn't a lot of fruits and veg shouldn't be a surprising one.[3] What is surprising, though, is just how fascinating that barren landscape is. Vivid, crisp sunsets paint the Mongolian steppe untamed shades of fire. There, the horizon is unchained, whipping up winds to swirl the dust and bend the faded stalks of dry grass that cling to life. Beyond the crowded capital is a landscape so untouched, so raw, you can't help but smell it in the breeze. A lofty silence calls the steppe home, the wind whispering secrets in a foreign tongue.

But this isn't a story about picturesque landscapes. This is a story about being polite, and the cross-cultural consequences that occasionally follow.

I had been traveling around Europe for a few weeks with my partner Christine before we hopped on a plane to Moscow. We were off to ride the Soviet rails across the largest country in the world, from Moscow all the way to Beijing. Our journey would take us through the heart of Mongolia, a heart that beats a parched and savage tune. We would spend a few weeks making the trip, though in hindsight (again, fucking hindsight!) I would have enjoyed at least another week, if not more. The overwhelming majority of that extra time would have been spent in Mongolia. Don't get me wrong, there is lots to see and experience in Russia but I was blown away by the uniqueness of Mongolia. It was clear, even after five minutes in the capital, that this was a land like no other.

Swirls of dirt and dust whipped around Ulaanbaatar, a city enveloped in enough smog to rival even a summery Beijing. The cars ceaselessly honked, horns being used where most other countries would use a turn signal. The cacophony stretched across the entire city, a web of tangled noise. The honks were warning signs of caution and anger, a habitual reaction in a country without rules of the road. As our senses adjusted to the chaos, we noticed that there were no standard car models in Mongolia. Every imported car was left as is, leaving some drivers to sit on the right and some on the left as they beeped their away across the city. The economic disparity was clear, too. Brand new cars jostled for space beside others that were as old as we were, the aged vehicles spewing dark smoke into the cool night air. It was all so new, so odd. I loved it.[4]

Perhaps if I had done my research I would have discovered some of these facts before I left...but I didn't, and I am eternally thankful for that. Without any preconceived notions or expectations, I was able to really see and experience Mongolia — its charms and its flaws — without a filter. The more I travel, the more I feel this is by far the best way to experience a new place.

The downside of not preparing for a new destination is that you will likely get lost in its unfamiliar geography — which we did, immediately upon arrival. We weren't lost in one of those quaint *we're-lost-BUT-look-at-all-these-neat-things-we-found!* kind of ways but rather in a *it's-midnight-and-we-can't-find-our-*

hostel-and-I'm-le-tired kind of way. Quantifiably less charming.

The directions I had scribbled down in my journal were vague and our linguistic proficiency was lacking, leaving us unable to coax adequate directions out of the few locals we passed on the street. A cab slowed as it drifted by, shouting to ask if we wanted a ride…or, I think that's what they asked. Chances are they could have found the place but we were stubborn and cheap so we politely declined. One disappointing hour later, we gave up the search and checked in to a run-down hotel near the train station. It was an overpriced and under-cleaned building that served as a tolerable place for one to catch a few z's…but hopefully nothing else.

We set out early the next morning a few bucks poorer and with a new-found determination to find our hostel. Our hunt took us in and around some of the more obscure neighbourhoods of the capital, offering up a chance to witness the daily goings on of life in Ulaanbaatar. We walked up and down a handful of streets, residential and otherwise, taking in the morning routine of the city. The daily commute was a commotion of sound, slowly fading in the distance as we left the downtown core behind us. After a few hours of exploring and searching, and with the generous help of a few kind locals, we were able to find our accommodation. It was tucked away in an unmarked back alley, the sort of place I wouldn't even have thought to look, so we didn't blame ourselves too much for our navigational shortcomings.

Upon arrival, we were warmly welcomed by the hostel owners, who immediately got to work helping us plan an adventure. They ushered us into their bustling abode, stepping over the countless backpacks that were scattered about the floor. Towering rucksacks, beat up and worn from their travels, were piled on every bed, chair, and couch. The remainder were leaning up against the walls, walls painted with a shade of off-white that had faded over the years to the colour of old bone or dying grass. It seemed fitting. Music echoed from the kitchen as travellers cooked up a generic storm of pasta and unidentifiable meat, a budget backpacker staple. A mix of accents chatted over food and maps, the rolling din edging toward boisterous. Settling into the hectic hostel, we plotted and planned our next few days, chatting with the other travellers who were doing the same. We swapped the standard small-talk questions with one another, trading stories and tips and misadventures. This is social kindling on the road, the building blocks of friendships that extend beyond cultures and borders. It's these seemingly benign (and oft-repeated talks) that bridge gaps; they are extended hands bringing travellers together, reminding us that we all have more in common than we think, regardless of what silly accent we have.

Though sometimes they are just awkward exchanges between strangers.

As the conversations played out, a young British girl interrupted Christine mid-sentence. Her British accent was thick and brimming with sass.

"You're from Sweden? You don't look Swedish." (Read: "You're not blonde")

Her tone was confrontational, and the conversation in the dorm came to an hush. Christine awkwardly chuckled and mumbled an incoherent reply, not really sure how to politely respond to the odd interruption. I could read her mind, though, as she bit back a crude retort.

You see, the British girl was black and she had rather nice teeth. Anyone can play the stereotype game.

Eventually the conversation rolled on, and we spent the night chatting with other travellers and catching up on emails. It was a nice change of pace from the quiet and contemplative train rides that brought us the 6,000km distance from Moscow to the Mongolian steppe.

We awoke before dawn to the stale smell of weary travellers. The odd bunk creaked and cracked as our roommates tossed and turned. Fumbling in the semi-dark, we packed our bags and stepped out into the lingering chill. Our guide was waiting for us, so we hopped into his beat-up jeep and weaved our way out of the turbulent city. The roads were empty, the humming capital catching its breath before another deep plunge into chaos. Dust kicked its way along the sidewalks as I watched, my face pressed against the glass to witness the birth of a new day. It wasn't long before we were free of its concrete clutches, escaping the smoggy urban sprawl to embrace the spartan steppe. Wide open space, as far as could be seen, greeted us. The grassy stubble stretched out on each side of the road, grey-greens and faded-yellows painted over arid browns. Watching the scene unfold, it became vastly apparent just how hard it would be to grow food here. Gardens were a rare sight, and the only trees we saw were those intentionally planted and maintained in a small National Park. What we did see, though, were rolling hills and flatlands stretching to the horizon. The sky itself loomed broader and brighter than anywhere I had ever been. We saw herds of camels roaming the dusty flats and some of the largest birds of prey on the planet being touted for tourists passing by.

We were not in Kansas anymore.

We bounced along for a few hours on what passed as a Mongolian road. From any uppity North American point of view, however, it was just chipped slabs of dated concrete more or less arranged in a semi-straight line. Within the first hour my ass was tender, my bones loose in their sockets from the jarring ride.

As we lazily cruised onward, leaving the city to fade into the smoky skyline, we eventually arrived at something a little more familiar: paved roads. I was slightly perplexed when I first saw their gleaming back outlines, for we were truly in the middle of nowhere. We had spotted nothing but sporadic Mongolian tents, known as *gers*, for miles upon miles yet a brand-new road now softly cushioned our tires as we sped along.

That's when I saw the gate.

Reaching up from the plains was a stark white archway that shone against the soft golden background of the steppe. Towering before us, as if conjured from a distant mirage, was a monument both shocking and epic, gleaming under the peerless gaze of a Mongolian sun. There, before our very confused eyes, was Chinggis Khan.

In the city centre of Ulaanbaatar there were some great statues of Khan, including the oft-photographed seated Khan who stoically overlooks the spacious central square. But this Khan was both incredible and ridiculous all at once. The statue was in the middle of nowhere — and nowhere in Mongolia is about as nowhere as you can get. We arrived as the only tourists in the vicinity, and we are talking about a building with a parking lot the size of several football fields. The statue itself was unbelievable. Immaculately crafted out of steel, the horse-riding Khan gazed out over his vast and distant empire. At 131ft tall (and on a 32ft base) it stood a vexing sight in the barren desert landscape. Of course, we had to go in.

The main floor had all the requisites of your standard tourist trap: mandatory tickets, trinkets and postcards, oppressively doting and pleasant staff, and a tacky dress-up area for photoshoots. We decided to pass on the photo booth and instead meandered toward the basement, where a museum was located. In the dim lighting, we gorged ourselves on the dramatic ups and downs of the past few thousand years in

Mongolia. We read about Khan after Khan, their conquests and failings, as soft Mongolian music kept the empty silence at bay. The displays were very well presented and maintained, though they were very much pro empire, never failing to remind us how badass and important Mongolia used to be. Point taken, Mongolia. You used to kick some serious ass.

After exploring the mini-museum we took an elevator up through the statue itself to a look-out platform on the top of Khan's horse...because what's a giant Khan statue without a lookout platform on the head of a massive aluminum horse? From there we could see for miles, an ocean of golden sand and amber grass sprawling out toward the limitless horizon. Dotting the scene were sporadic gers, mere specks upon the canvas. Looming behind us was the giant head of Khan whilst before us his former empire rested in majestic stillness, nothing moving but the wind as it danced briskly in our ears.

Our cozy time with Uncle Chinggis now complete, we drove out to a small village where we were invited go horseback riding.[5] Now, as a vegan I'm obviously not too keen on riding horses (or any animal) but I couldn't bring myself to argue the point. Here we were in a man's home — a surprisingly spacious yet intimate ger — with his family, his dogs, and his horses. We were his guests and he treated us with a welcoming kindness, so who was I to judge his lifestyle? Before an introduction to our equine companions, however, we were graciously invited to stay for lunch. I immediately felt uncomfortable.

As a stereotypically-polite Canadian who spoke no Mongolian, I was hard pressed to decline the offer, hoping a forlorn hope that at least part of the meal would be vegan friendly. I should have worked harder to find a way out of the invitation because lunch entailed a uniquely-odorous milk tea (known as *Suutei tsai*), kimchi, and meat dumplings.

Fuck.

I had dropped my vegan guard and now I had to pay the dietary price. This is the obvious downside when it comes to traveling with dietary concerns. My personal feelings toward killing are often at odds with the cultures I visit, making it difficult to soak in every facet of each locale. As a vegan, I've come to accept that I cannot really understand each place I set foot in, and that I will inevitably be skipping aspects of the local cuisine. I'm ok with that. I've learned to act as a witness where I cannot be a participant, peering into each cultural kaleidoscope as deeply as I can and leaving with as nuanced a snapshot as I can compose.

This time, however, I would be a participant.

As they brought out the food, I formulated a culinary escape plan that wouldn't offend my lovely hosts. I started by eating most of the side-dish, a spicy homemade kimchi. I devoured the small bowl as our guide and our host chatted, the children climbing about the furniture in the multi-room hut. Feigning to be full (I'm a pretty thin guy so it was somewhat believable) I declined their offer of seconds. But they, being good hosts, insisted, so there was no getting around this. Much to my chagrin, the host and his family had already eaten, leaving their attention squarely on us. They were curious about our reactions as we tried the local cuisine they had so generously prepared for us, watching as we smelled the steaming tea and the heaping plate of dumplings. I was prodded to take a helping of the meaty pockets and so I placed a few on my plate, smiling an uneasy smile as my brain kicked into overdrive. It didn't cross my mind at the time, but as I look back I have to wonder what kind of dumplings they were. Cows were few and far between in Mongolia, though it could have been imported beef from China. Doubtful, however, seeing as we were miles from anything that resembled a store. And while I did see several herds of camel, I don't think camel dumplings were a thing.[6] So it must have been horse meat. Hmm. So much for My Little Pony.

At their insistence, and with no escape in sight, I bit the cultural bullet. Jaw locked, I pinched a greasy dumpling with my chopsticks and brought it to my lips. It was still steaming, and the smell bordered on the unfamiliar. This was the first meat that had touched my lips in over eight years, and I was worried I would have some sort of psychological reaction — let alone a physical one — to the very act of eating meat. But it was too late to do anything but open my mouth and plop the bite-sized morsel on my tongue. My teeth pressed into the dough, gushing burning juice against my tongue and the sides of my mouth. I braced to vomit up the slippery and savoury bites, ready for my body to reject the experience in its entirety. But it didn't. So, I continued, and with a smile on my face to boot. It was an important reminder: sometimes, you just have to let go and accept the fact that you can't dodge the rain.

Here's to getting soaked!

Chopsticks in hand, Christine followed suit, stabbing a dumpling and inelegantly ripping it open with her teeth, letting it cool before she closed her mouth around the steamy pocket.

I continued my meaty escapade, chopsticks flicking a few more dumplings to their digestive grave.

OR SO IT APPEARED!

Rather, as they watched I pretended to enthusiastically stuff my face with the mystery meat. Whenever their eyes glanced away I subtly spat out what I could into my hand and slipped it into my pocket. I could feel the warm, greasy tidbits soaking through my pants as they dripped down my leg. It burned, but I worked to ignore the slimy sensation as we conversed as best we could in a mix of broken languages. As I coughed, hacking up the remnants that lingered on my tongue, I was politely reminded that I could wash down my

Seabiscuit dumplings with a sip of piping-hot milk tea.

Sigh.

The tea smelled burnt and bitter, an acquired taste I would unabashedly — but non-judgmentally — rather not acquire. Flailing in the cultural quicksand, I could not muster the desire to go any further. This is where Christine became my hero. She was vegetarian, so the foreign cuppa wouldn't affect her gut like it would mine. She downed her tea during our attempts at polite conversation and nonchalantly set the empty mug beside mine. I picked up her cup and pretended to drink from the empty glass while she picked up my steaming beverage and drank, unhappily. I could see that she was struggling, her belly brimming as she choked it down. She kept a smile on her face, a brave front as she finished her second cup. And like that, our ruse was over — successfully, I might add — and no one was noticeably offended.

That is, until our gracious and attentive hosts topped up our cups once more.

They were impressed that we drank it all — and so fast! We were forced to repeat our deceptive routine, switching cups when their attention was on their children or the fading embers of the fire. This is where Christine became a saint in my eyes: The Patron Saint of Wussy Vegans.

Another round of tea down, bullets mostly dodged, we thanked the family — who were incredibly hospitable and welcoming, don't get me wrong — and went to meet our noble steeds. As we walked out to the stable, I fed my pocket scraps to their dogs, who could smell that I had something hiding in my pants. They jumped and pawed at me as I flung the half-chewed bits into the dirt. At least someone enjoyed the dumplings.

We got saddled up, doing our awkward best to clumsily

prepare the horses from the instructions given in errant English. Alas, these were not the epic war horses ridden by the hordes of Khan as they pillaged their way across the globe. Our steeds were not massive nor particularly quick, more akin to donkeys than the battle-tested beasts of the former Empire. I was okay with that, though, as I sure as heck was no seasoned raider.

We plodded up to the base of the cliff along a gentle slope, leaving the valley floor behind us as our stout and indifferent beasts led the way, more familiar with the trail than we would ever be. The gradual slope transitioned into something far more steep as we approached the foot of a monastery, its stairs rolling down the hillside like the wrinkled trunk of an elephant. Wanting a closer look at the ancient temple, it was there that we left our guide and the horses, hiking the rest of the way on foot. A narrow trail snaked through the dry grass, leading us to the monastery steps. We climbed the faded grey stones, weaving between the stairs, a footpath, and a bridge before finally reaching the monastery gate. The wooden door was thick and old, painted in faded murals and designs that had been weathered away by half a lifetime's worth of seasons. A lone monk, toothless and robed, stood watch from the hilltop. He tried to hustle us for a few bucks, insisting we dress up and snap a few photos with him. We politely declined, choosing to spend our time soaking up the view. The bright and sharp blue sky was beginning to smear itself into a brilliant flurry of darkening oranges and reds, gushing colour into the ceaseless expanse above. Clouds eased into view, casting fragile shadows over the hills that surrounded us as the day bled itself into dusk. Aside from our guide and the monk, not a soul could be seen.

Satisfied with the view, we trekked back to our awaiting mounts. The steep descent was bumpy and slow and I was sure that I would tumble out of the saddle as we plodded down the slope. Either that, or that my testicles would rupture from the unnatural and agonizing angle. Christine, too, was having some difficulty.

Her horse decided it would blaze its own trail down the grassy slope, ignoring the safer route that myself and our guide had taken. Winding ever closer to a solitary tree, the lethargic beast trudged onward, closer still. Then, all of a sudden, she was too close. Without regard for its inexperienced rider, the horse went straight under the tree, ignoring the uncomfortable commands of the terrified woman on its back. My jaw both literally and figuratively dropped as I saw a low branch lining up to decapitate my Swedish BFF.

With superhuman agility and miraculous horsemanship, Christine dodged a branch that most certainly would have removed her pretty Swedish face from her pretty Swedish head. She threw herself backward, Matrix style, tossing the reins as she clutched the beast with her legs. Laying flat against the rump of her treacherous pony, she disappeared from view, only to suddenly spring back into the saddle after clearing the thick branch. Even our guide couldn't help but be impressed, laughing in surprise as he flashed her a thumbs up. He would make a Mongol of her yet.

(Understandably, she hasn't ridden a horse since.)

Arriving back at the hut, heads intact and testicles bruised, it was time to say our farewells. We still had a few hours of driving before we returned to the sooty city of Ulaanbaatar and night was fast approaching. Pinpricks of stars already poked through the navy-blue horizon, celestial precursors of the Mongolian twilight. The family offered us some food for the road but this time I managed to decline — politely, of course.

We drove off into the night as the sun died before our eyes, falling victim to the silky shadow that seeped in from the far-flung corners of the immeasurable horizon. Strands of light, like veins of life, retreated into the distance as once again we gave ourselves to the chaos of a concrete city sprawl.

~~~~~

It was three days later, in frenetic Beijing, when the dumpling remnants caught up with me. I spent a night and day hugging the toilet in what is still the fanciest hotel I have ever stayed in. Booked as a reward for us having both completed and survived our trip across Russia and Mongolia, I was never able to truly enjoy its luxurious amenities. In the middle of our first night, basking in the glory of a king-size bed, I awoke, unsettled. I dashed to the exquisite bathroom and shit my brains out. I proceeded to shit said brains out every hour for the next day; for over twenty-four hours I ran to that toilet and punished the polished porcelain with a merciless vengeance. As for Christine, the Patron Saint of Wussy Vegans, she spent that time enjoying the amazing and super-cheap room service, exploring the city, and shopping.

Karma, perhaps. And a lesson learned.

roaming, ever still
a brave heart sewn to a vagabond soul,
stray and brimming

Shit Happens

A Lesson in Cause and Effect

Freeing oneself from words is liberation
~ Bodhidharma

In 2007, I left university and moved to a Zen Buddhist monastery in Japan. I had been practising meditation for a couple of years in Canada before I felt it was time to make a serious commitment to my practice; university just wasn't doing it for me in terms of personal development and discovery. I searched for a monastery with the most rigorous schedule I could find, said farewell to my family and my partner, and hopped on a plane to Osaka. I fumbled my way from there to Okayama and entered monastic life. Within 24 hours I had a shaved head and was raking sand gardens with the best of 'em. The following story is from my time at the monastery, which was one of the most profound and incredible periods of my entire life. This story should demonstrate why.

I was nervous. While there was not a doubtful fiber in my being, I felt awkward and unsure of myself as I arrived. My mind danced around all the potential variables of the situation, grasping at mental straws. *What will I say? Will there be a door? Do monasteries have doorbells? Are doorbells even a thing in Japan?* My hair was already short, but not razor shaved. *Should I have shaved it before I arrived? What's the policy on that?* I had a million and one questions, all battling for attention in a mind that had no idea what to expect next. After all, it's not every day you move to a monastery.

Before me stood the heavy wooden gates of the monastic grounds, seated at the base of a small mountain in the bustling city of Okayama. A small city by Japanese standards, it was nevertheless a sobering challenge to make my way from Osaka to the temple. Knowing only a handful of Japanese words, it was touch-and-go as I harassed locals for directions, eventually stepping onto a bus that would take me into the suburbs of the city. I fumbled for the right amount of change, the heavy Asian coins still unfamiliar to the touch. Looking to the driver for reassurance, I pushed the coins down into the machine one by one. Even the *beeps* and *clinks* of the machine sounded foreign, a subtle reminder that I was on my own, alone on the other side of the world. Not a single person in this country — hell, on this continent — knew my name. I was nothing but an aside, here. A background character.

I sat down in the first row, keeping myself within earshot of the driver. I had scribbled some crude directions in Japanese and flashed them to him when I boarded. Whether he could actually make them out, however, was yet to be determined. As we bounced along, my eyes began adjusting to the unfamiliar: cars on the left, surgical masks obscuring faces, an incomprehensible language announcing bus stops. The only thing keeping the culture shock at bay was acceptance. Acceptance that I can only be *here, now.* That there is nothing to do but press forward.

After crossing the bridge from downtown and weaving further away from the city centre, the bus driver nodded to me that my stop was next. As the bus slowed, I glanced back to see rows of empty seats; I was officially alone. It seemed fitting, that emptiness. Noticeable and momentous. I was some 10,000km from home, smiling at a sharply dressed bus driver wearing immaculate white gloves. I stared at his hands as I absentmindedly shouldered my backpack. *A bus driver wearing white gloves. How odd.* I wondered what he thought about me. What would he have said if I told him my studies were postponed, my significant other was left to live her life without me because I wanted to come here? Would he have applauded my leap of faith? Would he have scolded me for making a foolish decision? I didn't have the guts to ask, so I stared at the door. If there was a time to turn back, it was that moment.

But that moment came and went like seasons: all to brief, yet seemingly eternal.

Tightening the straps on my bag, I thanked the driver with a polite half-bow, launching myself into the unknown. I stepped out into the suburban quiet, my lungs expanding in the humid air. Once a secluded monastery, the temple was now just another facet of the familiar sprawl that plagued every modern city. Following the questionably vague directions I had jotted down, I made my way up a narrow road lined by tall pines. Their fading shadows crisscrossed the sidewalk as the heavy trees loomed over me. They were the guardians of the temple, judging my very quality as I slowly approached the distant gates. Monks of old would have to wait days seated at a monastery's doorstep before proving their dedication and earning a seat in the meditation hall. I simply sent an email.

Stepping through the gates, I was transported back in time. An uneven stone path led directly to the main hall, cresting over a small pond filled with fat and vibrant koi. To each side were stark sand gardens, perfectly raked antitheses to the boisterous disorder the monastic gates held at bay. For the next several months this would be my home. It was another world, a peaceful war zone where monks would wrestle their demons, witnesses to the formidable depths of their own being. It was not, I came to understand, a place for the faint of heart. Monasteries are a training ground, a spiritual and psychological boot camp. Once you sit on that meditation cushion there is no escape — you cannot run from what arises. And what arises is *you*.

I paused just past the gate, drinking the bloodless silence deep into my soul…and then I stood around looking like an idiot. *Well, what do I do now?* I wandered about until someone happened to pace by. A young monk in flip flops, no doubt recognizing my confusion by the dumbfounded expression on my face, ushered me to the empty meditation hall. Apparently, I had arrived on a day off so most of the monks were still out.

Apparently, monks get days off.

I was given the rest of the evening to explore the grounds and adjust to my new home, to shave, and to figure out how to get dressed in proper monastic attire. By the end of the night I was bald and beautiful, decked out in a tattered kimono and matching skirt, known as a *hakama*. In the early dark of that first night I stumbled my way over the unfamiliar and treacherous cobblestones to the evening chanting of sutras and the assigning of tasks for the next day. I mumbled my way through the chanting, my eyes and brain struggling to process the sutra text as fast as the monks were reading it. Heads bobbed to the staccato rhythm of the Japanese text, the vibrating and monotonous sounds spilling out into the night.

As the next day's chores were announced, I heard my name, sharp and direct. I looked up as the head monk announced my job: I was tasked to empty septic tank of the guest house.

Welcome, Chris.

The chore was actually announced as "toilet dumping" which certainly made me wonder about the day to come. Curious as to what my task would entail, I prodded one of the more senior monks for details. The monk was in his sixties, a fast-talking Basque who had been living at the monastery for more years than he could count. Fluent in a handful of languages, they all seemed to intermix in his hasty reply, though I extracted the basics as best I could. During the morning work period, known as *samu*, I was to dig a hole in the forest floor to which I would then empty buckets of urine from the guesthouse. Hence *toilet dumping*. I was enthusiastic about diving into monastery life, even if it involved a subtle form of monastic hazing, so I accepted my task with a smile and a bow. I'm sure there is a quote from Buddha somewhere about accepting whatever life throws at you — especially if it's piss — so I shrugged it off and got to work.

When my shovel hit the dirt it was just shy of forty degrees, the humidity heavy in the lungs. Not surprisingly, digging a giant hole in an uncleared forest floor was a challenging task. In the crippling heat, I had worked up a sweat and decided to take off my shirt. Naturally, I didn't think twice — it was stifling and I was sweating Zen bullets so the shirt had to go.[7] Alas, being that it was a co-ed monastery, and, well, that it was in fact a monastery I was given a polite warning by a passing monk that I had to stay fully clothed. I held my tongue, holding back what would have been some subtle mix of shade and sass. As an adult, I wasn't used to people telling me what I could wear, and it was an interesting feeling letting that go, giving up some autonomy for what could be called the greater good. After some reflection, it seemed a more reasonable request, so I donned my robes once again. Unfortunate, but ultimately understandable. Monastery life wasn't supposed to be easy, anyway. And besides, a little heat stroke never killed anyone.

After a few hours of hacking and hauling I finished the work, drenched in both sweat a few splashes of piss. I may have smelled like I just swam in a pool of ammonia, but I felt productive. Manual labour has that rewarding quality of seeing the immediate products of your effort. I could see where I started, what I accomplished. My sore back and sweaty brow were evidence of my effort. It was all right there, in the moment.

That was day one.

It wasn't until a couple months later when I was given that same opportunity to "feel productive" again. Toilet dumping was once more on the daily work schedule and this time it was for the *zendo* — the meditation hall. The *zendo* is where everyone sits in meditation, which for us was usually between 6-15 hours per day. It is also where the men lived, sleeping in a communal hall side by side. It took some getting used to (mainly because dudes snore and I'm a super light sleeper) but it was actually something I learned to appreciate. It came remind me of a children's book I had growing up — Peter Pan. We were the Lost Boys, and the *zendo* was our tree fort, our refuge, our Neverland.

In addition to the fact that toilet dumping was for a larger building this time, it was for also for both, uh, number one and number two. Myself and a few other lucky monastics were literally going to be hauling holy shit. I confess, however, that I was less enthusiastic this time around.

The toilet dumping crew consisted of myself and some of my monken comrades, each donned in soilable clothes. The septic tanks were located around six feet below ground, built into the side of the temple. The plan was for us to scoop everything up with a long ladle and dump the contents into plastic buckets. We divided the work into scoopers and carriers — those who scooped up the slurry into the awaiting buckets, and those who shouldered it to the pits dug in the wood — and set to task. It wasn't the best way to spend a morning but we were all in high spirits and saw the task through...with only one minor, messy, and surely inevitable hiccup.

Thanks to my long and lanky limbs and general lack of upper-body strength, I was tasked with being a scooper. I scooped bucket after bucket, whittling away the hours as the tank was slowly but surely emptied. As I scraped the bottom of the tank for the final dregs of excrement, two of my shit-hauling friends arrived with what was sure to be the final bucket. The hole we dug was already overflowing, the compostable sludge seeping into the forest that would soon consume it.[8]

With the last bucket full to the brim, the two monks began a slow shuffle as they balanced the bucket toward its woodland grave. They had only made it a few feet before the ropes abruptly snapped, breaking free of the bamboo that rested on their shoulders.

Eyes widened. Time itself came to a shocking standstill. The bucket fell in slow motion, giving us all enough time to contemplate our messy fate. The bucket landed perfectly perpendicular to the cold, hard dirt. The jarring force flung the cocktail straight into the air, arching away from the monks who were, just moments ago, hauling it to its final resting place. Miraculously, not a single drop touched either of them, nor did any fly my way. It was a miracle.

Sort of.

It just so happened that one of the monks who had the day off was doing his laundry barely a few feet away from the wayward bucket. His karma was different.

The sludge found its target over *and* through a nearby lattice to where said nonchalant monk was washing his clothes, enjoying a rare moment of leisure time. In less than an instant he was covered in shit; head to toe, he stood a brown monument to our disastrous calamity. He froze, in unadulterated shock, as our slow-motion reactions collided with reality. We all stood, mouths agape, shouts of warning uttered moments too late. We could do nothing but wait for his reaction and the heavy silence lingered, wordless and colossal.

And then I heard my name. It was said with the utmost calm,

yet firm enough to bend my will. I hesitated, but eventually replied, leading him to provide me with one simple instruction:

"Go get my camera."

I ran, realizing the potential future joy this moment would bring, and grabbed his camera. I snapped a handful of pictures before he trudged off to the shower, laundry in tow. The rest of us started to clean up the mess, still in full and utter appreciation of his stoic response.

~~~~~

One of the foundational pillars of Buddhism is the Four Noble Truths. The First Noble Truth is often translated to *"life involves suffering."* I like to think that can roughly be modernized to *"shit happens."* Since it will inevitably happen you might was well relax, snap some pictures, and enjoy what you can, when you can...because you never really know just when you'll find yourself covered in shit.

Bloodstains on the Banana Pancake Trail

A Lesson in Patience and Priorities

In the summer of 2014 I packed my bags and moved to Sweden. Technically, I was still waiting for my residency permit so I couldn't stay in the country long. Hog-tied by red tape, the bureaucrats informed me that I would wait up to 11 months for my paperwork to process. Not content to spend that time in cultural limbo, my Swedish partner Christine and I decided to spend that time traveling. With our bags packed and tickets bought, we hopped on a plane to Asia for some adventures along the Banana Pancake Trail.

Our bus broke down. It shouldn't have been a surprise, considering its dilapidated exterior, the pockmarked roads, and the questionable sobriety of the drivers.

Drivers. As in plural.

For whatever reason, we seemed to have been assigned a second driver for our trip, even though the duration of our journey was but a few hours. The two men were pushing the boundaries of middle age, as well as the outer limits of their belts. Like our ride, they had both seen better days. Wrinkled and grey, their tanned skin was a dark shade of bronze oh so similar in colour to the bottles of beer they dubiously sipped as we waited to board. Nursing their drinks under the ungainly whirl of a low-hanging ceiling fan, it seems they were committed to knocking back a few cold beers before we departed the station. Admittedly, some folks seem to perform better with a bit of booze in their system, and as I climbed onto the bus I held a hope that these gents were those kind of folks (functioning alcoholics…with the emphasis on *functioning*).

We were on our way north to Bangkok after soaking up the sun on the diver's paradise of Koh Tao and its boisterous neighbour, Koh Samui. We diligently dodged the inebriated ridiculousness of the Full-Moon Party, indulging in a more low-key island life. Our fellow backpacking bus mates, clad in vibrant muscle shirts and airy elephant pants, were notably less diligent. Rows of sweaty twenty-somethings filled the seats around us, the conversations a mingled mix of accents. Sun-burnt skin, in varying stages of lobster bright to half-peeled and shedding, was common. A few lucky passengers also wore the backpacker badge of honour: bedbug bites. On the odd shoulder or exposed calf, I could trace the pestilent lines, unattractive remnants of an unlucky feast. I'd survived over a year in Asia without so much as a single bite, but I knew I was the exception to the rule. (Christine, her bad luck a constant source of entertainment for me, was not so lucky) Bedbugs and sunburns were but par for the course in South East Asia.

We had been on the road for the better part of three months, our bodies acclimatized to shitty bus rides and the low-budget lifestyle that forms the foundation of backpacking. Every day was a Saturday, an excuse to chill out, wander, stuff our faces, and generally just do whatever tickled our fancy. We were living the backpacker dream, basking in our unchained freedom with only a few hiccups along the way to keep us in check.

About an hour or two into our ride the bus came to a rolling stop along a busy highway. We had, not surprisingly, broken down. With no air conditioning to keep us from boiling, everyone piled out. Keeping to the unpaved shoulder, the

Full-Moon Crew mingled along the side of the highway, snapping duck faced updates for their Instagram. It should go without saying that snarky complaints highlighted the entire process. Over the din of conversations, I heard the crack-hiss of a few beers being opened. It must have been lunchtime.

As for me, I tramped out into the brush away from prying eyes and took a piss in the bushes.

After draining a pair of Changs — the budget-friendly go-to lager in Thailand — with practiced speed, the drivers held a brief conference. After some mumbled discussion, the two wheelmen nonchalantly decided they could not only find the problem, but fix it — whatever *it* was. They grabbed a rusty toolbox from under the front seat, opened up the trunk, and began to examine their project.[9] Now, I know nothing about engines so I can't begin to fathom what was wrong but from the looks of things something just needed to be replaced or maybe just tightened. At least that's what I gathered from their pointing, humming and hawing. That *something*, however, was located at the rear of the engine. It was, much to their sweaty chagrin, more or less unreachable. Someone would have to climb onto the steamy engine and crawl into the belly of the beast. The lucky mechanic would then need to hang themselves upside down, leaving their feet dangling out of the vehicle to tickle the humid Thai air. Then, they would have to locate the problem and go to work. Obviously, it would require someone nimble and thin.

For whatever reason the noticeably larger of the two men decided he would be the one to fix it.

He grabbed a tool so rusty it stained his hands, sucked in his gut, tightened his belt, and slide up and over the engine, disappearing into the semi-dark of the cavernous bus-trunk-engine-place. I stood around watching him as the rest of the young adults relived their recent Koh Whatever glory days.

After a few minutes of tinkering, the mechanic/driver seemed to have gotten things working. He shouted a muffled order to his co-driver, who then ambled back to the front of the bus — another Chang in hand — and started the engine. Voila! He was able to MacGyver whatever it was that needed MacGyvering and got that shit fixed. To be honest, I was both surprised and impressed. If it were me, I would have just walked the 150 meters to the fatefully-located car garage that we had serendipitously broken down near and asked them to deal with it. So, kudos to the drivers for their initiative/frugalness.

With the engine coughing back to life, everyone began to eagerly pile back on the bus. I lingered near the rear just to make sure the engine didn't crap out before I got back to my sweaty, AC-deprived seat. In part, I didn't want to clamber back on only to have to clamber back off should their tinkering be found lacking...but I was also mildly concerned for the driver still half buried in the engine. Fortunately, the engine didn't quit.

Unfortunately, something worse happened.

The engine chugged an uneven tune as it heated back up. With the sputtering motor having been on for a few moments, the dark smoke that poured from the tailpipe transformed into a softer shade of toxic grey. As the familiar petrol perfume leaked into the breezeless air, I noticed that the rotund man pinned upon that engine was struggling to wiggle himself backward out of the motor-trunk. The problem was — and he didn't know this at the time — that there was an exposed belt (seriously, there was just some kind of exposed conveyer belt propelling this machine?) spinning rapidly beneath his bare and calloused feet. Those very feet, had he continued to lower them, would have become a mangled mess of broken toes and shredded muscle; no amount of callouses or leathered skin would have saved him from that outcome. But he didn't know that. He was just starting to freak out because he was stuck on a burning hot motor and couldn't wiggle free, cooking alive in the engine-oven. I'd be flipping my shit, too.

He started screaming in Thai, a language incomprehensible to me. Screaming in terror, however, is sort of a universal language in and of itself so I caught on quick. I rushed forward before his toes nicked the belt, another young backpacker doing the same. We grabbed the man's legs, supporting his ample weight as he shimmied himself toward us. Propped up on my shoulders, I could smell the stale sweat and warm beer that oozed from his greasy, sooty pores. His legs flailed as he inched toward us, his knees catching me in the chin and chest as we worked to lower him toward the ground. We struggled to pull him loose as he in turn pushed himself free, our arms wrapped tightly around his legs and waist as we strained to keep him — and ourselves — from dipping toward the spinning belt. It didn't take long before he was out, which was fortunate because neither of us could have supported his expansive frame for much longer.

Back on solid ground, he looked terribly relieved. Surprised, but relieved. I don't remember the word for "thank you" in Thai but he said it half a dozen times as he struggled to catch his breath. Bracing himself on his knees, he pushed back a thin lank of thin, grey hair that clung to the droplets of sweat on his brow. He knelt there, chest heaving, adrenaline pumping. After a moment, he stalked up to the front of the bus to fill in his clueless fellow driver on what the fuck had just happened. Leaning against the driver's door, he cracked open a beer and lit up a cigarette, a well-earned reward for this tinkering.

A young Aussie decked out in a bright pink muscle shirt and matching sunnies gave the man a slap on the shoulder.

"Well done, mate. Fackin' legend."

Refreshed and recovered, the driver sucked the last life from his smoke as he loosened his belt back into the realm of comfortable. Tossing the butt into the dirt at his feet, he wiped his greasy hands on a rag before climbing onto the bus.

He gave me a nod as I shuffled back aboard, his shirt stained bloody and black from a few cuts and a whole lot of engine grease. Of course, I happened to be wearing the most expensive shirt I owned (it cost a whole $30) and it, too, had become stained with his blood and grime.

But I guess thirty bucks is a fair price to pay for helping someone not die.

Midnight Bombs in Sverige

A Lesson in Post-Apocalyptic Preparation

I awake to a terrifying noise. It's blasted through the room, echoing off the walls on repeat. It sounds nuclear, the sort of alarm one might expect to hear before the imminent detonation of an atomic bomb. I'm wearing ear plugs but I might as well be pressed against the speaker. The sonic onslaught has my heart pounding, my brain swelling with confusion.

It's just shy of 2 a.m. and I'm in a dorm room in Stockholm. The world, I assume, is ending.

I've already leapt to my feet, shimmying into my oh-so-tight H&M jeans as I nudge the last gasp of sleep from my bloodshot eyes. I don't bother with my flip-flops, letting my bare feet press against the cold floor as I reach for my wallet in the semi-dark. My backpack is already slung over one shoulder, all my necessities (read: my computer) safely contained. The other backpackers — an eclectic bunch from half the world's continents — are all sitting up, dazed and confused. Understandably so.

I take a leap of faith and presume the Atomic Bomb Alarm is actually a fire alarm, though why the Swede's chose this diabolical tone I know not.[10] I pause, upright beside my bunk, and wait. Chances are the building isn't on fire, though I'd rather not wait too long to find out. The sun barely sets in Sweden at this time of year, which means there is enough light leaking in from the uneven curtains to guide my way as I pace toward the door. A groggy Aussie, whose head is ear-bleedingly close to the speaker, starts clambering down his ladder. He's likely still drunk, having just got in from the bar, and he stumbles to the door in a pair of boxers reminiscent of those I wore as a teenager: unflatteringly baggy and unattractively plaid. He sticks his head out of the room, though no dancing flames nor plumes of smoke are to be seen. Someone is out there, though, a shadow in the fallout, and they exchange words with the half-naked vagabond. All I hear are the muffled echoes of their conversation as I wait, adrenaline pumping.

The alarm stops buzzing just as the Aussie lets go of the door; I never hear it slam thanks to the ringing in my ears. A fire drill? False alarm? Either way, it's over. No mushroom cloud. No End of Days. A part of me, I confess, is disappointed. I was already planning eight steps ahead, my mind racing through all disastrous possibilities. *Could I escape out my window? What food is there in my bag if I had to survive, trapped in a collapsed building? If I got caught up in a nuclear disaster/ building fire would blogging about it be inappropriate?*

More pressing questions, like, "Is there a fire extinguisher nearby?" fail to even register.

For whatever reason, I've always found crises fascinating. I won't go so far as to say I wish for them, but I certainly get a rush out of facing a dire situation. The higher the stakes, the more I feel alive. There is nothing extraneous involved, it's just you and the issue; everything superfluous falls to the wayside. You see the core of someone — usually yourself — in a crisis; you get to witness the heart of humanity when things hit the fan...for better or for worse. That, in part, is why I love to travel: because life on the road usually involves more crises than life at home.

I remember one of the clearest moments in my life occurred

during a crisis. I was a teenager, walking home through a wooded park when, out of nowhere, two cars started following me. They began with a slow crawl toward me, inching along a secluded gravel path. One followed me on the road and the other angled in from the side. It was around midnight in a town so small you could spit across it, making their arrival immediately suspicious. Creeping forward, their lights washed over me, forcing me to squint against the bright beams. Their tires crunched the gravel with a quickening pace, their speed increasing.

I was alert from the get-go, my guard already up.

After the slightest pause, the cars geared into motion. The rev of the engine was my cue: my legs started pumping. I sprinted down the gravel path before sidestepping into the woods. I dodged between trees and hid in ditches, slinking away from their high beams as they sped towards me. I danced around the vehicles, my backpack bouncing and bobbing as I ran for my life. I hid behind a tree; heart thudding, lungs gasping, brain razor focused.

One of the cars roared off the road and into the grass, crushing branches and leaves as it hunted. It weaved every which way, the lights searching for any sign of me. My only exit was a nearby fence. It would be a mad dash of 200 meters, but the cars wouldn't be able to follow. I tightened my shoulder straps. And then I ran.

Leaping over a muddy pit, I managed to slide under the gate to safety before I met my end. I was covered in mud and water, my pants ripped and dirty. My knees were cut, and my elbow bruised from a run in with a low branch. The cars stopped just short of the fence, their headlights lighting my final sprint to safety. I had survived.

And it was a hell of a rush!

For some twisted reason, I look back on that night as a fond experience. I've been hooked on crises ever since.[11]

Tonight, however, is just another fire-free night. I begrudgingly count my blessings as everyone starts to collapse back down into their surprisingly-comfy IKEA beds. I peel off my jeans, unsling my bag, and plop myself onto the mattress. So much for my beauty sleep.

Everything seems extra quiet in the aftermath of the alarm. No air-raid sirens wail in the distance, no blitzkrieg bombs hurl toward Earth. *Maybe the world has already ended...*

Wide awake, I glance over at my co-worker, tucked into the bottom bunk beside mine. She's fast asleep, dozing through the apocalypse. She never even woke up.

I suppose I need better ear plugs.

Piss and Stardust

A Lesson in Spontaneity

It should go without saying that a lot can happen in seven days. This is ever so dangerously compounded when Las Vegas is involved. Few people escape Sin City unscathed, for there the siren song sings *ad nauseam*, perpetually luring the uninitiated down the glitzy road to perdition. I was one of the few — very few, no doubt — visiting that stifling city of glitter and light who avoided most of its morally ambiguous smorgasbord of vice. Sure, I played with some machine guns, and yeah, I won enough money in poker tournaments to pay for my entire week-long stay at the Monte Carlo...but guns and gambling are just par for the course in Vegas.[12]

After a few days of guns, poker, and sweltering by the pool in the savagely intolerably 45-degree heat, I decided that it was about time to do something else. Anything else. When the cement gets so hot that it hurts to walk to the pool you know it's time for a change of scenery — and I'm not just talking a new set of slots.

I was in Vegas for a family wedding, which went by swimmingly. With the wedding — and its preceding bachelor party — out of the way, I found myself with a few days to kill after the ceremony was complete. On a whim, I reached out to some couchsurfers who were also visiting the city with the hope that we could kindle some sort of adventure. It was, after all, Las Vegas. There had to be *something* for a sober vegan Buddhist to sink his teeth into, right?

Having answered the call, I met up with three other wanderers late one night down on Fremont Street, the glitzy casino corridor of old Vegas. It was sometime after midnight when we gathered in a seedy bar that managed, against all odds, to stay dim amongst the chaotic glow of the bright city. Between the four of us we had four countries — and four continents — represented: Canada, Sweden, Russia, and Uruguay. It was a true couchsurfing gathering, a ragtag collection of vagabonds from around the world united by their desire to connect, to explore, to adventure. It didn't take long after our brief introductions to realize that there was, in fact, an adventure to be had — a particularly grand one, at that. The Grandest of Canyons was but a stone throw away, and it was something we all wanted to experience. Being the adventurous (read: impatient) types we didn't want to wait. We left immediately. By then, it was almost 1 a.m.

We pushed our way through the buoyant crowd, shoulder to shoulder with a thousand other night owls who aimlessly wandered the tourist trap, feasting on the lights and sultry chaos of a city built on chance. Squinting against the seizure-inducing sparkle, we hunted for a cab as 80's cover bands and celebrity look-alikes touted their desperate wares. Bottled water was hawked at every street corner in paltry defence of the sleepless desert heat. A zip line baptized tourists, two by two, in the gaudy radiance of American sin. If desperation had a heartbeat, it was there, greedily pumping tainted love and manufactured lust into the lost souls of the modern world. The extravagance, much like the smell of cigarette smoke, was overwhelming. We jumped into the first cab we saw.

Within minutes we were renting a car, breezing through the bureaucratic hurdles in record time. By 1:30 a.m we were buckled in, inaccurately GPSing our way along an empty freeway burdened only by construction. We promptly stopped for snacks (I don't go anywhere without snacks) and headed out into the pitch of the desert, hearts pumping with excitement to the blaring pop music cranked out over the FM radio. Our hastily considered destination was the South Rim, a mere five hours away somewhere in Arizona. The plan? Drive in pairs — one driver to drive, one to rest. One co-pilot to, uh, co-pilot, and one to sleep uncomfortably sprawled in the back. I took the wheel right off the bat, for no sleep would have me now. I was seized by the journey, energy drinks coursing through my veins keeping the sandman at bay as I chipped away the miles in Uncle Sam's backyard. My co-pilot was the wandering Swede. We chatted away the first couple hours while our Russian and Uruguayan comrades caught some shuteye in the back. Being complete strangers, there was a lot to talk about.

We traded stories and histories, genuine and honest, as we ploughed into the thick darkness of the arid desert. It wasn't long before we made a brief pit-stop along the side of the highway so I could empty my bladder of the growing number of energy drinks I was swimming in. A few hundred kilometres away from the noise and light pollution of Las Vegas, we were now enveloped in somber quiet seemingly empty of all sound. The shimmering canvas above shone brilliant, lighting up the desert around us. A black and blue ceiling cascaded above with more stars than I ever thought existed. Standing there, alone in the dark with what seemed like the entire universe above me...I was stupefied. I felt so small, so insignificant and alone. And yet somehow at the same time I felt intimately connected to *everything*. The adrenaline that coursed through my veins gave way to serene acceptance, calm and boundless. I could feel the cosmos, lightning under my skin. The sky loomed so heavy, so low it seemed within reach, as if I could simply stretch out and pluck each shining pinprick from the heavens and swallow it whole. I could already taste the stardust.

All this, and I was still pissing.

I can pee for a very long time.

Bladder empty, and my marvelling at the majesty of the universe now complete, we hit the road once more. Our collective goal was to arrive at the canyon by sunrise, having decided this for three specific reasons. First, obviously, was so that we could snag some epic photos. Second, so we could dodge the traffic and get a sweet parking spot. And third, to beat the heat. Arizona in the summer is an unforgiving environment, and no one in their right mind wants to hike in a desert in unnecessarily-oppressive heat.[13]

Our timing was perfect on all fronts: we grabbed a great parking spot, witnessed the birth of a new day rising over the expansive horizon, and started our hike before the skin-melting heat took hold. Flawless Victory.

Within the first ten minutes of our steep descent we had already lost our Russian companion. She disappeared off into the brush to blaze her own trail, refusing to simply stroll along the boring ol' path like the rest of us. Plodding into the canyon, I kept pace with the athletic Swede as she stalwartly trudged downward at an impressive clip. I was sweating bullets already and our Uruguayan friend, owing to a few extra pounds, was already lagging behind; he stopped quite often — and quite reasonably — to catch his breath and drink some water. The hike down to the two-mile point, while sweaty, was uneventful...which is precisely how I like my desert hikes. We stopped for water, shade, and to take in the incomparable scenery. The sun had barely inched over the horizon and I could already wring the perspiration from my thin shirt, leaving a small pool of salty liquid in the dust at my feet. Our wayward Russian was still nowhere to be seen, leaving us to linger a few extra minutes, desperately clinging to the breezeless shade. Against the reasonable discretion of the park signs, we fed the crumbs and scraps from our food to the gathering rodents as we waited...but the Russian was ne'er to be seen. We were left, then, with the invigorating challenge of hiking back up the canyon, a task our Uruguayan friend was — quite reasonably — not looking forward to. Clear droplets of sweat lined his brow and collected on his patchy beard as he gathered himself to follow my footsteps upward. I simply followed the Swede, ants marching onward.

After a sleepless night fuelled by adrenaline and energy drinks the hike began to take its toll. Our pace slowed as we dragged our heels back to the top, the sun beginning to bake the very earth beneath our feet. It was then, just shy of the summit, that our Russian friend came crashing out from the bushes. She had a handful of cuts and bruises for her trouble, a toothy smile plastered on her dirty face. She was, quite clearly, pleased with her exploring. The daring endeavour left her covered in dirt and dust and sweat, an inevitable combination that left her arms and face blotched and smeared. It was the unintentional war paint of her sojourn and she wore it with pride.

Once more at the ridge, we took the time to enjoy the view. We had earned it, the beauty of it all increased ten-fold by our exhaustion. The panorama was unrivalled, vast and primal, like a snapshot of a world untouched by the greedy hands of mankind. There were endless shades of red and brown, my eyes blinking away sweat to spy the layers of bastard colours. The tacky postcards at the nearby gift shop were an insult to this view, utterly failing to convey the sheer immensity and awe-inspiring wonder of the scene before us. A wonder, I can assure you, that is infinitely sweeter with a parched mouth and a sweaty back.

At the top, we drank our respective body weights in rejuvenating water, cool and clean and life-affirming. Bellies full, energy spent, we nestled into the grass for a brief cat nap...which quickly evolved into a full-on sleep. Under the warmth of an August sun, we slept the day away, blissfully content to be immobile as the crowds came and went. It wasn't until a few hours later, well into the afternoon, that we finally came to life, slowly stretching out to test the limits of our recovery. Reborn, refreshed, and inevitably sunburned, we casually made plans to visit the Hoover Dam on our way home. It was time for our adventure to continue.

It didn't take long for us to get back on the road, our spirits lifted and our music roaring once again. This was our home. We were all wanderers, travellers to the core, and we were in our element: a lone road, a mission, new places and spaces to witness and explore. We were kindred spirits seeking an unfiltered glimpse, however brief, into the heart of the moment. We were each seeking the unfamiliar, chomping at the bit to feel, to connect with the world around us.

But first we needed to have lunch.

We stopped at a small, rundown diner in some one-horse Arizona town. It was your generic horror-movie locale: a rusted-out gas station with its lone mechanic, a dilapidated diner with a staff stuck in the 1980's, and a permeable awkward *nothingness* that enveloped it all. I suppose the rustic charm was lost on us, though that didn't stop us from scarfing down some fried delectables. I didn't want to press my luck and ask if they had a veggie burger (for fear of being axe murdered) so I settled with some fries and enough ketchup to keep the uncomfortableness at bay. The frumpy waitress, sporting a rather drab ensemble that matched the dreary ambience of the hideaway, and her grouchy hash slinger eyed us curiously as we ate; an act as amusing as it was unsettling. Suffice it to say, with such a warm welcome and inviting atmosphere we didn't stay long. Intent on leaving the eerie pit-stop behind us, we traded jokes en route to the highway. We were all in agreement that this was the exact sort of place one hopes they never get stuck in, a Silent Hill shanty town that likely saw our tires slashed to prevent the escape of fresh meat.

Well, the truth wasn't so far off.

Within a few moments of being on the highway we heard an explosion. We all jolted upright, rocked in our seats as our speed suddenly dropped. Wide eyed, we exchanged worried looks as we lost what little acceleration our small rental car had to offer. It was happening: we would be axe murdered. Or cannibalized. Possibly both. This was America after all. Anything was possible.

I fumbled to find the hazard lights and pulled onto the shoulder. We checked each of the tires for problems/knife marks but it seemed there was only one that was in questionable shape. And by "questionable shape" I mean it was ripped open and shredded. We looked over our shoulders, waiting for the perpetrators to appear, chainsaws in hand. Squinting into the distance, we saw nothing but buzzards.

As we later discovered, the sun — giant fireball of exploding plasma that it is — caused the asphalt on the roads to heat to such a degree that our tire overheated and popped as soon as we got back on the baking highway.

But we didn't know that at the time.

Unsettled, an eerie quiet hovered over us. We had a spare tire, fortunately, and between the four of us we were able to see the job through with basic competence, though admittedly it took longer than it should have. With the new tire secured and its ruined predecessor sitting pretty in the trunk I made a mental note that I should really learn more about cars before my next trip. A lot more.

Unfortunately for us, our spare tire wasn't a proper replacement: it was a "donut," a tire not meant for long distances nor particularly fast speeds. This meant we couldn't even reach the posted speed limit as we hobbled along back toward Vegas, a distance the spare tire might not even survive. Just like that, our five-hour return journey exploded into a reluctant eight-hour marathon. It seemed, much to our collective disappointment, that our chance to see the Hoover Dam had burst with the tire. Nevertheless, we escaped the murder town unscathed (which is always a plus in my book) and made it back to Sin City under the cover of darkness, safe and sound and sun kissed. We returned our car without a hassle, having bought extra insurance at the behest of our Uruguayan co-adventurer. As we returned the car and keys, the employee seemed completely indifferent to our mishap, which I took for a good sign. He informed us just why our tire had burst, as well. So much for axe murderers.

As we flagged down a cab to get back to our respective hotels it suddenly dawned on us that our Fellowship was ending, almost as abruptly as it began. Once more on Fremont street, we shared a brief but heartfelt farewell. I watched each of them disappear into the dry and morally ambiguous night air toward adventures yet unknown.

As for me, I had to take a piss.

this sacred empire
built on the lost art of losing your way
fueling the piss and stardust with maps for
kindling
fires on fires
burning compass lines in the snow
seasons for stamps, we'll fill this book
our sacred empire

Christopher Kevin Oldfield

The Bunkless Bunk: Zen and the Art of Hostel Etiquette

A Lesson in Being Discrete

Buddhism makes mind its foundation. It makes no-gate its gate. Those relying on words, trying to strike the moon with a stick, scratching a shoe because they have an itchy foot —
what concern to they have with reality?
~ The Gateless Gate

There is a man watching me have sex. Or, I think he is watching. In the semi-dark of the curtained dorm room it's hard to tell. He is definitely probably listening. Craning my neck, I can see that he is propped up in his bunk — a bottom bunk perpendicular to the one I'm in — clicking away on a laptop. The screen casts an eerie glow over his half-hidden face, flickering shadows into the dark of the room. I peg him to be in his early twenties, and even though I've seen him on and off for the past day and a half I have no clue where he is from or what he is doing in the German capital. He hasn't mumbled more than a few words in that time, and has rarely even left the dorm room. I'm hoping he has headphones in, though I wager they wouldn't do much good; the high-pitched grind of creaky, cheap metal is unavoidable.

Focus, Oldfield.

Here I am in the middle of having sex with an incredibly attractive young woman and all I can think about is the emotional well-being of the unidentified backpacker no doubt stealing glances at my sub-par performance. I suppose it's my own fault for having sex in public.

Now, I like to think that, generally speaking, I make good choices. My parents raised me to be considerate and polite and respectful and I can confidently say that, generally speaking, I am. I also don't drink alcohol which, on average, helps prevent me from making poor or embarrassing life choices. But average isn't always.

My visit to Berlin marks my first time on the continent, and after initially being approved for a two-month holiday from work I've ended up with "only" five weeks, forcing me to reprioritize all of my travel plans. The days and weeks leading up to my flight from Toronto to Paris were spent tediously reviewing and adjusting my route, having been forced to completely cut the Camino de Santiago from my itinerary. *Next time*, I tell myself. It's a slippery slope, "next time." I've seen, first-hand, the consequences of letting opportunities slip from grasp, moments unseized. I've watched "next time" become the passive mantra of too many folks who unwittingly let life escape their clutches. Nothing kills dreams like the disease of tomorrow. "Next time" is terminal, and I'm never a fan of embracing it out of anything but necessity. Earning an income, unfortunately, is something of a necessity.

After a week-long tourist binge in Paris I've come to Berlin with no real plans other than to explore the once-divided city and stuff my face with as much vegan grub as my wallet can afford. Pretty standard. It's early October but the weather offers up a summery vibe. Bright blue skies and a warm sun are the unseasonal backdrop to my short walk from the bus stop to my hostel...a hostel that I can't seem to find. I spend fifteen minutes wandering back and forth along the busy street convinced it should be within sight yet blind to its actual location. Somehow, I've talked myself into believing that if I keep scouring the same area over and over again it will appear out of the blue. It doesn't, and I make a mental note to scribble down better directions next time…though I'm already sure that I won't. Inconvenient as it may be, I like getting lost. It's in those unfamiliar spaces where we are most vulnerable, most open. Our expectations are left behind, clinging to the sign post as we press into a new expanse. Sure, it can be tedious and annoying at the worst of times, but at the best of times it is a refreshing change from the expected.

The world is vast and wide. Why do you put on your robes at the sound of a bell?

I continue to stumble around, double checking my map as I hunt through my notebook in search of additional tidbits of information. It's 2012, long before Google Maps becomes the traveller's BFF, and I'm left to just be lost. My foreignness is blatant but generally ignored on the semi-bustling sidewalks, people coming and going from cafes and convenience stores, living their lives as if I wasn't even there. It's an odd, yet reassuring, feeling when you realize just how minuscule the sphere of your life is. To the man on the corner selling aromatic currywurst I am no one; to the woman peddling flowers in the parking lot of an unknown church I basically don't exist. To them, and most of the world's population, I am just nameless face furnishing the landscape. I am the backdrop, an obfuscated shadow on scrim. In a way, this is the ultimate freedom. There is a rare sense of limitlessness you can only find in a new place, and only if you let go of yourself and your expectations. I bask in it.

Even in the subdued urban chaos it's easy to see that Berlin is a lush city. Flowers and parks and trees and grass are never far from view, breathing fresh life — quite literally — into The Grey City. As I drag my heels about I eventually notice a partially-obscured side street. Poking my head around, I decide to wander a few blocks off the main road, just because. This is the freedom of traveling without a plan: you can just do whatever. There is no pressure, no schedule. If you want to explore, you can explore. If you want to sit and people watch, you sit and people watch. I'm hard pressed to think of a greater sense of utter freedom.

If you are unable to find the truth right where you are, where do you expect to find it?

As luck would have it, my aimless wanderings lead me to stumble into the hostel within moments — though it's nowhere near where I expected it to be. It's a rather large building, some four floors or so, built into a block of old, unflattering apartment buildings. The drab and chipped concrete complex is a stark contrast to the bright autumn leaves that are dying all around me. They are pretty reminders that I've made the right choice in coming here, in taking the leap and making the most out of what little time I have.

After checking in, I tramp up to my dorm, a spacious room host to a dozen steel bunks, each wobblier than the last. Hardly ideal, but the hostel was chosen for its price and its location, not the quality of its IKEA bed frames. I'm fortunate that it's the low season and my dorm is practically empty. The scores of noisy kids on class trips are stomping about a few floors below and I pray a secret prayer in thanks. For company in my commodious dorm I have a reclusive backpacker of unknown origin who is rarely seen without his laptop. I don't recall seeing him leave the room for more than a few moments, constantly hovering over the keyboard doing Lord knows what. Otherwise, it's just me…and eventually a female companion. But she comes later — pun intended.

What did you look like before your grandparents were born?

After seeing the sights, hearing the sounds, smelling the smells, checking out the vegan stores, and getting lost a handful of times, we're back at the hostel — me and my female companion. It's nighttime, and while I want to say late it's probably around 9:30 p.m. Hell, it could even be 10 p.m. — I like to let my hair down when I travel. We decide to put on a movie, having watched one the night before as a wrap up to a tiring day of exploring the city on foot. This time, we're crammed into her bunk, perpendicular to the pale backpacker who is still clicking away on his laptop, having not yet left the dorm for God knows how many days. All I can see is the white-blue glow of a computer screen reflected over his bespectacled face in the attempted dark of the quiet dorm. I assume he is working, or perhaps apartment hunting having just moved to the city. For all I know, though, he could be watching hentai while browsing Neo-Nazi forums so I don't bother to enquire.

Squished together in the single bed, we're sharing earbuds, watching The Patriot or some similarly-generic action film that I have no qualms admitting to liking. The previous night it was Jurassic Park.[14] It's the travel equivalent to "Netflix and Chill" long before that was even a thing. Like your stereotypical Netflix and Chill one thing leads to another. I'll spare you the Grade 10 anatomical review, though this is no mere foray to first base — I'm rounding third and on my way home. Unfortunately, but not surprisingly, the trip to home base is an awkward one. The vampyric backpacker is a mere ten feet away and we don't have a curtain. The creaky, wobbling bunk isn't helping.

As I work to make a good first impression, I not-so-subtly steal glances at the glowing backpacker of unknown origins (Ok, I'm thinking he's German?) to make sure he isn't noticing. We never make eye contact, but he must be able to hear; as quiet as we are, he must know. Can he see precisely how pale my ass is in the semi-moonlight, or are we just flailing shadows, an awkward mystery his eyes can't decipher? Every time I get back to the task I feel his focus on me, drilling holes of judgement. He HAS to be looking. I mean, I would be. Be honest, you would be too.

When you can do nothing, what can you do?

My commitment to the task is dwindling, eroded by equal parts hilarious embarrassment and a healthy dose of Canadian politeness. We're both trying not to laugh at our predicament, but between trying not the creak the bunk, trying not to hit my head, choking on the musty scent of a stale hostel, and while trying to enjoy the experience...well, it's not happening. This, I conclude, is why people get drunk. Unable to continue under the watchful gaze of our forced voyeur, we decide to end our midnight foray into more than just friends. And so, we stop, smiling and giggling about it like children. Weird, semi-perverted children.

Years later, respectable hostels will begin to attach curtains to each bunk. I suppose you could say I'm something of a pioneer. You're welcome..

A Cobra Named LUCY

A Lesson in Close Calls and Long Calls

I didn't expect to see so many bones.

Stark white specks, picked clean by the beasts of the Maasai Mara, dotted the landscape. The off-white remnants were never far from view. A thigh bone by the road, a shattered skull near a watering hole. The fragments salted the plains, an ode to the perpetual struggle of life here in Africa. Some were still fresh, decaying in the clingy African heat. I spied the half-eaten corpse of a dead giraffe, still upright, predominantly untouched. Hunched over and rotting, the bottom quarter of its body had been gnawed away, it's head, missing. But the torso was intact, like a totem warning us to stay away. Its colour had faded to a blurry shade of muddy brown, the bright yellows and oranges lost to the elements. It smelled the way only dead things can smell, pungent and clawing.

This is Africa.

Breezing past zebras and impalas, I watched the savannah stretch out toward the distant horizon. Morning was rolling in, leaving the plains deceptively cool. The hazy orange bulb above us was inching its way from behind sepia clouds, breathing fiery life into the world. Bouncing along, cameras flashing, a pair of cape buffalo didn't even bother looking up as we passed, indifferent to our intrusion. They chomped at the trampled tufts of grass at their feet, a sea of green broken only by other animals — both dead and alive.

As our van kicked up dust along the makeshift road, we spotted movement in the distance. Our driver snatched the radio from the dash and mumbled something in Kiswahili, muffled replies echoing in response. Shifting gears, he clipped the outdated walkie-talkie back on the dust-covered dashboard and stepped on the gas.

We came to a rolling stop after blazing across the expanse, joining up with a handful of other safari vans. Before us, sitting majestic upon an outcropping of stone, was a male lion. He was still young, though a darkening mane encircled his thick neck. He looked proud, in a deserved way, his place above us well earned.

I had never seen a lion up close, not like this. Even at the zoo, you'd never get too close to the beasts. The lazy bastards would always stay at the back of their cage, away from the gasping, prying masses and their ever-encroaching selfie sticks. And I don't blame them. If shitty humans kept me in a tiny cage I'd do the same. Seeing them in the wild, though, was something completely different.

We rolled closer, inching our way into his domain. We weren't more than a dozen feet away by the end, toe to toe with a creature that could have killed us all with a decidedly miniscule amount of effort.

But he didn't move.

Sprawled on a rock, he just laid there in the dusty breeze. Sometimes he watched us, sometimes he looked around, uninterested in our existence. After snapping a dozen or two photos, I set my camera down to watch, unfiltered. That's when our eyes met. I could tell he was more than just watching. He was judging. Calculating. He was not only looking at me, but through me. Past me. As if I barely existed. I could feel his power in that gaze. Confident and palpable. Present.

And *free.*

There was an aura of calm around him, of purpose. He emanated a feeling of simplicity, one that was quite mesmerizing. Dozens of us stood around, just watching him, engulfed in his presence. It was almost hypnotic.[15]

It wasn't long before the radio squawked and our driver was informed of another sighting, but of what we had yet to find out. Excited to see what else the park had in store, we buckled up and sped along the trail. I watched gazelles and topi mingle with zebra and wildebeests as vultures circled above, waiting for their next meal. As we came into a clearing, however, it became apparent that this gathering was no ordinary affair. Something was wrong.

Parked in the middle of the dirt road was a safari van with its doors open. Surrounded by other drivers and tourists, the van sat there, engine off, hood popped. A crowd of onlookers had gathered.

I stood up, shifting to look through the open space in our roof. Beside me was a broad-shouldered Aussie, bearded and husky. We strained to make out what was happening, listening to the chatter as we took in the scene. Neither of us spoke Swahili, but we could read the situation that was painted on each driver's face: something bad had happened.

...or was happening?

...or was about to happen?

Really, we didn't speak a word of Swahili so it was hard to tell exactly where we were in the timeline of this brouhaha. It took a few minutes of eavesdropping before the blanks were filled in and we caught wind of what was happening. One word stood out to my ears, rising above the indecipherable Kenyan language to ensnare my attention.

Cobra. There was a cobra.

I scanned the scene as my brain processed the new information, digging up anything it could remember about cobras.

…which was nothing. Countless hours of watching BBC documentaries and I couldn't remember a damn thing. Hm.

And that's when I saw a driver splash water into his eyes, hastily emptying an entire 1L bottle directly into his sockets. He was a big guy, cresting over six feet with his head shaved razor clean. He took a knee, chest heaving, as he wiped his face clean with his shirt.

Curiosity piqued, I whistled to our driver, Peter.

"What happened? Why are they stopped?"

"No problem. Just a cobra. It spat in his eyes."

No problem?

First off, I didn't know cobras could spit. I made a mental note to keep that in my back pocket for trivia nights/future life and death situations.

Second, no problem?

Clearly my threshold for "no problem" needed to be re-evaluated.

With our safari van locked from the outside, we were confined to quarters. Under most circumstances, this is for our own safety. Situated in a vast and diverse biosphere full of deadly animals — including lions and, apparently, cobras — it was generally considered for the best if the patrons made it home alive.

But I wasn't in the mood for safety.

I propped myself up on a seat, using it to give me a boost as I scrambled through the safari sunroof. I shimmied down the side of the van, absorbing the fall with a feeble shoulder roll. Dusting myself off, I noticed a few broken fragments of bone at my feet. I didn't take that as a good omen.

Darting back to the van, I opened the sliding door to let the other passengers out before stalking up toward the cobra car.

It seemed the driver — now in the throes of going blind — saw a cobra on the road so he decided to stop so his passengers could snap a few Insta pics. Photoshoot complete, he then drove onward, passing over the cobra. When he looked in his rear-view mirror to make sure the cobra was still alive, it was gone. As the car rolled overhead, the tricky son of a gun decided to crawl into the carriage as it passed, curling up for some cozy R&R in the engine. When the driver got out to investigate, he popped the hood. That's when the cobra spat venom in his eyes.

Why he would drive above the cobra is beyond me. But that's hindsight. Lesson learned, I suppose.

Looking to avoid a confrontation with the gathered crowd, the snake burrowed its way into the engine, lodging itself in quite snuggly. Thick as my forearm and longer than I am tall, it was somehow able to tuck itself into the nooks and crannies with relative ease, basking in the extra heat and warmth that radiated from the outdated motor.

The downside to this whole debacle — in addition to someone going blind, I suppose — was that the half a dozen passengers whose van was commandeered now had no ride, and all their possessions were stuck in the cobra car.

It was, as my Aussie companion pointed out, "A bit of a hiccup."

With a broom handle and some sticks collected from the

bush, the drivers took turns banging on the front of the car, hoping to coax the snake out by means of their racket. Too stubborn to rest, the half-blind driver joined in, himself banging on the bumper with a dry piece of wood. The park rangers had already been called and a medic was on the way, but we were far out in the bush and the consensus was that they wouldn't arrive any time soon. And so, they banged away with their sticks.

When the engine banging proved futile, our ingenious collective of safari drivers had another bright idea: smoke it out.

How? By starting a fire under the van.

...yeah.

Grabbing some rags, rubber, and wood, the drivers carefully made a pile under the car, pushing the items under the engine with the broom stick, covering their faces to avoid any more venomous sprays. Doused in gasoline, they lit the pile ablaze.

Or tried to.

The wind that whipped along the plains kept putting their fledgling fire out, forcing someone to awkwardly run up, re-ignite the fire, and then run away, face half covered.

Not only was it tedious, but it was dangerous. We were, after all, surrounded by hundreds of miles of dry, flammable grass. I tried to politely bring this up but was waved off. The half-blind driver wanted his revenge, and no uppity white tourist would get in his way.

After 10 minutes of stoking the fires, it was clear the snake would not be bothered. The crowd was puttering away, losing interest but unable to leave — their drivers were invested in getting this snake out of the car. Seizing the moment, our driver Peter dashed into the van and turned it on, revving the engine. Warming up after a few moments, the snake began to shift; it was getting a wee bit warm for its comfort. Revving the engine over and over, the snake started to look for an exit. Within a few minutes it was free, curling over the edge of a worn tire before slithering into the knee-high grass.

The crowd cheered, applauding our driver, now the hero of the day. Steven, the venom victim, clapped the man on the back, his eyes red but his vision holding.

It was a close call.

Excitement over, we hopped back into our van and rolled along the flats, parking ourselves in the shade of a lone tree. Small lunch boxes were handed out from the back of our van, the sides of each cardboard container slick with grease. Shaking off a dusty *shukka*, the traditional Maasai blanket, Peter sprawled it out in the grass. I plopped myself down, greasy lunch in hand, looking over my shoulder into the tall golden grass bending in the breeze. *If there was a lion there, would I see it? Would I hear it?*

Probably not.

Hunger overpowering my desire not to be eaten by a large cat, I pried open my lunch. I was assured that a vegan lunch would be provided by the tour company, though clearly their definition of "vegan" was different than mine. Inside the box was a piece of dried out chicken, an egg sandwich with a few mystery ingredients, cookies, and a juice box. Oh, and an orange.

Salvaging what I could (the cookies were vegan!), I offered up the rest to the other passengers. Lounging in the dirt, I let my eyes take in the cloudless expanse above. My stomach was rumbling, but I figured it could be worse. At least a cobra didn't spit in my face. (Plus, I had cookies!)

We spent the rest of the afternoon bouncing around the park, taking in one epic sight after the other. We spotted a rare black rhino trudging its way along the savannah, watched lion cubs wrestle in the shade of some brush, and listened to an exhausted cheetah enjoy the fruits of its labour, a sound I will never forget.

(If you've ever wondered what a cheetah sounds like when it is eating a freshly-killed wildebeest, the answer is that it sounds like a wet cotton t-shirt slowly being ripped at the seams. Yeah.)

As we gorged on the visceral rarity of it all, I noticed my stomach was starting to knot. Little pins of pain shot up every time we hit a bump, which was every other moment since we were usually off road. I mentally walked myself back over the lunch, wondering if there was something I ate. And then I did the same for the previous night's dinner. *Was there some water I drank that was questionable? Did I get stung by something and am on my way out?* My mind worked over the possibilities, though it was clear something was amiss.

Within the hour I was clenching, my guts ready to thread themselves through whatever exit they could find. We were, quite fortunately, already on our way back to camp. A mere twenty minutes out, I was sure I could hold it until we arrived.

I was sure, that is, until I wasn't.

Whatever the issue was, it was clawing to evacuate my feeble frame, and I was diligently working to prevent it. My stomach was tight, tensed from flexing, my brain razor focused on not shitting myself. It escalated quickly, and within moments my brow was dotted with sweat. This would be a photo finish — if I was lucky.

Pulling into the camp of the Aussies who were with us, I dashed from the van, awkwardly intruding into their conversation.

"Sorry guys, I don't mean to intrude, but do you mind if I borrow your bathroom?"

Fuck, why are Canadians so polite?

In true Aussie fashion, they were accommodating, ushering me toward their cabin. Engine running, Peter stuck his head out of the window and shouted to me.

"Will it be a short call or a long call?"

I gave him a stupefied look; my head cocked, toes clenched, as I pondered that he meant. *Will it be a number one or a number two?*

Realizing the question — and slightly surprised that it was shouted publically — I looked at him: my pale face said it all. Stepping out of the van, he lit up a smoke while I clenched my way into the spacious cabin.

The Aussies were gracious enough to wait outside while I collapsed on the toilet. There was no real door on the bathroom, just two broken saloon flaps that offered the merest shred of privacy. There was no toilet paper to be seen, either, though I couldn't actually see much because the lights didn't work. But it didn't matter, because my body had already given up.

I sat there in the dark for 10 minutes. By the end, the toilet was — quite literally — full. It was also, I discovered, broken.

I jiggled the handle, but it wouldn't flush. I tried again, a bit more frantic. Nothing.

Fuck.

Wiping the sweat off my face, I yanked off the lid to see if I could manually flush the thing, fumbling with the parts to no avail. Embarrassment was knocking on the door, and if I didn't find a solution I would have to answer. I pulled out my phone, using the light to examine the toilet, but it was beyond my unskilled abilities.

After a few minutes of tinkering, I gave up. The toilet wouldn't flush and now their bathroom smelled worse than a dead giraffe. I stepped back out into the light, physically refreshed and reborn, ready to embrace my shame. Squinting as my eyes adjusted to the light, I waved over the burly Aussie.

"So, uh…funny story. The toilet won't flush and, well, it's not pretty. I…I don't really know what to do."

Without skipping a beat, he slapped me on the shoulder and broke out laughing.

"Don't worry, mate. Ya'see, the thing is, I messed up. That's not our cabin."

I could only reply with a furrowed brown and a look of utter confusion.

"Yeah mate, our place is over there, the one that says LUCY."

He grabbed me by the shoulder and turned my body as I glanced up, shading my eyes with my hand as I scanned the cabins. On a faded canvas wall, I could see LUCY crudely painted, in all caps, in bright green spray paint.

The gravity of the situation hit: I had just destroyed, beyond all question, the livability of someone's accommodation by filling their broken toilet with a slurry of bowel sludge. Wow.

I started shaking, overcome by a laughing fit so fierce that it seized my muscles, tensing my entire body. The Aussie chuckled, shaking his head, his face as red as mine. We both lost it, half-collapsing to the ridiculousness of it all.

Glancing around to make sure that no one was looking, we made our exit from the now-ruined abode and headed back to the van. *Should I have left a note? "Sorry for ruining your cabin. Sincerely, some random tourist who isn't even staying here."*[16]

Our driver Peter waved as I approached, peeling himself off a bench to head back to the van.

"That was a long call, my friend."

"And a close one, Peter. And a close one."

Christopher Kevin Oldfield

This Is Not The Way

A Lesson in Misplacing One's Sanity

"They've tricked us! They've TRICKED us! There is no town! We're not going to make it!"

She is in tears, her face red from the sun and the panic that has suddenly gripped her. Her shoulders heave, rising abruptly and jagged. Her feet drag, momentum lost to the growing despair that tightens in her chest as she chokes back further tears. We are in Spain, somewhere in the expansive central plateau known as the *meseta*, hiking the ancient Camino de Santiago: The Way of Saint James. We ran out of water hours ago and dark specks now sail the skies above, unknown birds of prey awaiting the moment when their next meal — that would be us — keels over. The sweltering and shadeless plains have left Christine to bake herself into delirium. As for me, well, I'm simply doing my best not to laugh.

Owing to its repetitive scenery, unbearable temperatures, and lack of amenities, the *meseta* is a section of the Camino many pilgrims skip. Filling the geographical void between Burgos and Astorga in Northwestern Spain, I find it to be one of the most stark and stunning landscapes I have ever seen, rivalling the empty beauty of Mongolia and the arid, limitless vistas of Arizona. Immeasurable blue skies are our constant companion, as are the golden fields that line the flats, enveloping our narrow trail. It is already early September yet the temperatures staunchly cling to the mid-30's as summer refuses to make way for its seasonal successor.[17]

We're just past the halfway point of our 800km journey, our pace a clear indication that we've finally come into our own. My feet, disgusting as they are, have hardened to their purpose. The single blister that left me limping a few days past is now nothing more than a flap of dying skin clinging to a calloused toe. Christine isn't so lucky; she has blisters on her blisters, her feet riddled with the bulbous and burning liquidy lumps.[18] She has nevertheless kept a steady pace, refusing to give in to the torment though a grimace has been etched into her sun-kissed Swedish face since day one. She has already gone through four pairs of footwear, yet none have provided more than a few hours of reprieve from her painful predicament.

Today, however, blisters are a secondary concern.

Under the cover of a lukewarm dark we awoke in the village of Población de Campos. Getting dressed in the pitchy shadow had never been easier, a familiar routine on the *Camino Francés*. Like most anything else, it all came down to preparation: my headlamp was waiting for me on my sandals, which were precisely aligned and tucked under the bed; my bag was packed the night before and my hiking clothes hung from the worn bed frame; my water bottle was already full and my walking stick and boots eagerly awaited my arrival out in the hallway. My wallet and phone were in my cap, wrapped in a sun-faded bandana I bought for €2 in Pamplona, its predecessor lost to the immutable winds that endlessly batter the Pyrenees. Over the past two weeks this ritual has evolved from a clunky and vague *fumbling* to its current swift and polished form. Within moments I was dressed and packed, a silent and organized *peregrino* on his way to Santiago. The lazy Spanish sun wouldn't rise for two more hours, and so we tip-toed our way out of the *albergue* and into the refreshing air of a brand-new day.

This day was set to offer a rather unique challenge, for somewhere during the 35km hike ahead of us was a 16km gap wherein there would be no towns or villages, no water, and virtually no shade. Our guidebook described the section as a "scenic treadmill" — hardly reassuring. Before we could worry about that treadmill, however, we had to remember how to walk. With over 400km notched into our weary bones even the simplest of tasks required some initial concentration and effort.

To begin, I simply eased my way into a slow amble as I reacquainted my body with the art of walking. It was half hobble, half swagger, my un-oiled joints loosening as we paced our way through the dark. My knees and hips were weary and stiff, seeking out that ever-familiar rhythm. Encased in heavy boots, my chafed feet thudded into the ground with a dissipating limp. My gait evened out after a few hundred meters as my calloused hands found their familiar grasp on my walking stick. It was a relic from France and the very first day of our journey.

That was a lifetime ago.

Since then, I had bonded with the stout and weathered stave. It had become my saviour, the friend I leaned on when times got tough. It was an extension of my effort, of my very existence on the Camino. It connected me to the earth with every footfall and to the sky with every twirl and toss. For whatever reason, I named it Jefferson.

As the sun began its tortoise-like crawl into sight, leaking light and colour across the horizon behind us, a dirt path led us toward Revenga de Campos. There we paused for the briefest of moments, guzzling a few cold sips of water as we breathed deep the silence of another day en route to Santiago. The silence was just as cold, just as restorative, as the water that sustained us. It was a spiritual necessity.

We pressed on to the slow clicking rhythm of Christine's walking poles as they stabbed into the packed earth. Even after the merest pause it took time for our bodies to re-acclimatize to the act of walking. It goes without saying that pain — often considered penance — is an integral part of The Way, and it is never more acutely felt than after a break. While walking, your body and mind adapt to the varying degrees of discomfort. That pain and discomfort are boxed in and held at bay as, step by step, you battle your way to Santiago. When you pause, whether for the day or simply for a splash of water or a glance at your guide book, it's unleashed. In stopping, that discomfort is let loose and it requires an admirable degree of patience and dedication to box it all in again and continue.

But sometimes you can't.

Sometimes you just hit the wall. Your feet won't move. Your joints burn. Your shoulders ache, your back folds to the strain of carrying your own weight, let alone the additional weight of a 5-10kg backpack. This is why a growing number of pilgrims hire companies to carry their bags from hostel to hostel. It's a controversial service, one that forces us all to consider just what the Camino — what a pilgrimage — truly is.

For us, the Camino is a challenge: physical, mental, and spiritual. For us, one must carry their own baggage, both literally and figuratively. Under the right (or more accurately, wrong) circumstances that challenge overwhelms us. It crashes through the gates of our perseverance and reminds us of both our toughness and our fragility as human beings. The Way will show you your flaws...but if you look deep enough it will also remind you of your strengths.

Those strengths were replenished in Carrión de los Condes, our last stop before the treadmill gap. We filled up our canteens and chatted over our options in the shade as we grabbed a quick bite. I rustled out some semi-stale bread and olives from the day prior, carelessly stuffing my face as we discussed our dilemma: do we press on through the gap without a break, or do we rest and then tackle the expanse? As we mulled it over I watched an unknown bird of prey listlessly glide in and out of view, an indifferent witness to our pilgrimage. As the bird floated onward into the distance we agreed to do the same. We decided to push on into the gap as the temperature was only going to rise. There was, we reminded ourselves, a reason the *siesta* exists.

Stale bread devoured, we continued our march west and into the gap. The difference was non-existent.

Blue skies still painted the ceiling above, varying shades of yellow and gold and brown still highlighted the fields around us. The terrain remained flat and shadeless. Change, we realized, was generally slow to come on the Camino; the devil, as always, was in the details. Blisters only bubble with steady friction, shin splints only throb with mounting stress, water bottles only deplete sip by sip, and unprotected skin only sizzles red under a persistent sun. Lost in the haze of our own thoughts, in the rare beauty of our environment, we let the details slip.

Within the first hour our water was gone. When I licked my parched lips all I could taste was sweat and sunscreen. My bandana was soaked through, and Jefferson was slick and glistening from my sweaty palms whose unflagging grip had polished smooth the dead wood. The scorching sun directly above us now and it weighed heavy and oppressive on our shoulders. The last drops of Christine's water were lost to a sudden spill when, beneath the sparse bows of a rare tree, ants began falling from the branches to bite her neck and back. She dropped the water out of surprise, scurrying from the shade as we cursed its pesky inhabitants, once again captives to the Spanish summer sun. The *meseta* was transforming into a sauna. We had no choice to press on.

Another hour dragged by, though I refused to feel anything but carefree enjoyment regardless of how much chafing was occurring. We were neck deep in the challenge, battling the elements and ourselves. And I was loving it. Every step brought us closer to our destination, to shade and a cool shower in some village whose unfamiliar name I'd long forgotten by that point. More importantly, however, every step brought us toward a better understanding of ourselves. All we needed to do was embrace the journey and keep moving, slow and steady. I blinked away the sweat that perpetually trickled into my eye, the slight sting a mere annoyance as I fluttered my eyelashes in meagre defence. I was unable to wipe the sweat away for there was no part of my outfit that wasn't drenched; I could already wring the perspiration from my shirt and watch it evaporate in the dirt at my feet. It reminded me of my farming days in Canada, of slogging away at tedious chores under a sun that never seemed to tire...but it will. A sunrise necessitates a sunset, and all we needed to do was outlast the burning ball of hydrogen and helium that taunted our very existence. Admittedly, it was an uphill battle.

Christine was starting to slow. Half a foot shorter than me, she was always having to work harder at keeping up. I was perpetually in awe of her pace as she *click-clicked* her way forward, walking sticks jabbing the road in time with her feet. More than her flagging momentum, however, I began to see worry on her face. Her perseverance was slipping, that boxed-in discomfort was wriggling free.

"Shouldn't..." She was breathing quick, shallow breathes. "Shouldn't we have been there by now?"

Doubt was creeping in as she glanced over her shoulder to see if any other pilgrims were in view. She sought reassurance but there was none to be had. It's true that we hadn't seen another person for hours, but our early start had no doubt left them all behind us. We just had to keep walking forward.

Hold fast. The map indicated that there was a village ahead, though we had no clue precisely how much further. Another hour? Two? We simply had to continue, trusting in the guidebook and, dare I say, having faith in The Way.

Another hour passed. We were officially baking in the oven of the *meseta*. My mouth was so dry I couldn't even spit away the salt that pooled along my upper lip, the droplets of sweat clinging to my two weeks of prickly stubble. Christine stopped yet again, turning around to peer backward, squinting into the distance for any sign of life beyond our own. I simply stared up into the endless blue abyss, shielding my eyes from the clawing light. Not even a wisp of cloud to be seen, though I saw buzzards circling high above, no doubt awaiting our demise. I chuckled to myself, though in the back of my mind I wondered which of us would get the last laugh.

"Are you SURE this is the right way?"

Her voice carried frustration, exhaustion, anger, worry. It was a crisis of faith...more accurately known as heat stroke.

She started walking again, though her walking poles weren't *click-clicking* against the paved road. They dragged, screeching in protest as her arms hung lifeless at her sides. Her jaw was quivering, her brow furrowed.

"I don't think this is the right way. I...I don't think we're going to find the village..."

I found the whole situation absurd, though I did my best not to laugh at her alleged conspiracy theory. The sun was cooking her alive, her confusion the onset of heat exhaustion. I calmly worked to reassure her that we were on the right course, for there really was only one road that headed in this direction. Beyond that, there really was only one way to Santiago: the way you take. I kept my philosophical reflections to myself, though, walking beside her in hopes of keeping her committed to moving forward.

But the weight of the present moment catches up to her. She breaks.

"They've tricked us! They've TRICKED us! There is no town! We're not going to make it!"

She stops again, her legs giving in to the delirious terror and confusion. Tears sweep in to mingle with the sweat that dances along her face as the panic takes hold. She peers into the distance ahead but all there is to see are the varying silhouettes of the mirages that line each horizon. No clues nor hints at how far away our destination lay are present. I urge her to carry on, that we can take a break just over the next ridge. It's a lie, of course. At the next ridge, I will create another fictional finish line to lead her to until, eventually, we arrive at our nameless destination. I try to coax her forward but she resists. So, I up the ante, going so far as to convince her that our very *albergue* is likely just over the next ridge.

"We are pretty much there," I say, "so let's just get it over with."

She mumbles an incoherent response but her feet begin to move. Inch by inch, we continue. All rhythm is lost, her pace is off, arms moving with a lacklustre determination as she babbles nonsense. She is fuelled, now, by desperation alone and I worry that she will collapse when we get to the ridge and discover the inevitable nothingness that awaits. Forlorn, I look once more to the buzzards.

For the next few hundred meters we shimmy forward together, limping at a snail's pace. And then, suddenly, I hear laughter. It takes me just a moment too long to realize that it is mine, that it will no longer be the buzzards who get the last laugh. Poking through the distant mirage is the village, Calzadilla de la Cueza. We have, hilariously, survived.

Christine looks relieved beyond all measure, and her pace steadies ever so slightly. We carve out the final kilometres with a vengeance, basking in the glory of our makeshift victory. I can't help but flash the circling predators a sardonic smile as we approach the ridge. In Calzadilla, we shower away the layers of salt and stink, quench our immeasurable thirst, and relax in the shade of an *albergue* patio. Christine, far from recovered, slinks off to puke while I simply kick back and order myself a vegan *paella* and an ice-cold — and well deserved — Fanta.

I spend the next 10 minutes waiting, watching the birds of prey as they breezily swoop across the azure canopy, hunting for food in the nearby field. My meal arrives, though something was obviously lost in translation: I'm presented with a "vegetarian" *paella* curiously topped with half a dozen jumbo shrimp. Too exhausted to protest, I pick the seafood off and toss it into the field.

It seems the buzzards get the last laugh after all.

in a far-flung land
flushed green with kindness
I find myself, uncoiled
a solitary man
unraveled in the silence of a foreign sea

A Greater Town for Dying

A Lesson in Consequences

When I called home, I had nothing much to report. My trip was one amazing adventure after another, with only minor hiccups to spice things up and colour the background. I was simply calling to check in, to let my family know that I was alive and well. I was being a responsible son.

A bright Asian sun shone down as I leaned into the shade of the pay phone, filling in the details of my trip to my dad. It wasn't until I had spewed up my yoloing that he started to tell me what was new back home. And it wasn't good. My grandpa was sick, and was staying with him until further notice. The precise nature of the illness wasn't conveyed, and for whatever clueless reason I didn't press for further details. He was, after all, old. Old people get sick, no big deal. After a moment, the conversation shifted back to more pleasant ground before I hung up, departing once more to hunt down some adventure. I would be heading off the grid for a few days to refresh, to slow down and disconnect. No internet, no pay phones — just beaches and maps and campfires, bugs and sunburns and B.O. The simple things. The things that remind us that we are human beings, that we are universal and unique.

A few days later I got back to a hostel and checked my email. My grandpa had died.

He passed away in the Greater Town of Napanee,

surrounded by family during his final days. I suppose that's one of the better ways to go. But I wasn't there. By the time I could get to an airport and book a flight across the ocean I would have already missed the funeral. I was coming home in a few weeks anyway, so my family encouraged me to stay.

So I did.

As my family arranged and attended a funeral, I fluctuated between moping on the beach and moping in a dorm room. Here and there I battened down the emotional hatches and enjoyed the long hours of foreign sunshine and reflective strolls down the hectic streets of Naha, Okinawa.

Contrary to popular belief, there are downsides to traveling. And I'm not just talking about jet lag and sporadic nausea, not just food poisoning or bed bugs or squat toilets with no toilet paper. Beyond the financial cost, beyond the environmental impact, there is an emotional toll long-term travel extracts. While travel may be a privilege, that by no means makes it without consequence.

The moment you leave home, *you are leaving home.* Life will continue without you. Things will change, people will move on. Over time you may be replaced in your relationships by people who are present. For many travellers, this might actually be a plus. If you are coming from a toxic environment, this sort of escape might be a blessing. And that's wonderful — live it up! For those of us who come from families we love, who have friends we care about deeply, then travelling comes with a hefty price tag. Time may stand still for you, as you globetrot and bask in the quintessence of life, but it will sustain its onward march for everyone else. Or maybe you will grow and change in leaps and bounds, while life back home remains constant. In either case, you'll miss birthdays and weddings, births and deaths. Family get-togethers will proceed in your absence. You will start to grow apart from the life you led, and all those in it.

This is the price of exploring, of geographic and cultural curiosity. Are you willing to pay it?

~~~~~

Exactly twenty days before my grandpa died I mailed him a postcard. I don't know if he got it.

The Ice Cream Man

A Lesson in Kindness

Kumejima. You probably haven't heard of it. I'm not saying that to sound cool or well-travelled but because it's pretty much unknown to most the world. Located off the coast of Okinawa's main island, its claim to fame (if you can call it that) is a bout of ancient seismic activity that left a string of strange, lava-cooled stones around the island. Beyond that, like many places in the world, nothing terribly noteworthy has happened there. And by no means is that a bad thing. Kumejima is just a place where regular people live regular lives, ignored by annals of history. More often than not, those are my favourite places to visit because the onus is on *you* to discover the charm and beauty of the place. The information isn't handed out in guidebooks or reviewed on travel blogs; it is there, in the moment, where you must discover the character of a destination. In that regard, Kume was no exception.

To get there, we left Okinawa on a hulking and aged ferry. The rusted vessel ploughed through the waves for a few hours, the constant churning and dropping leaving me queasy. Out at sea, the dreadnaught swells were towering and indifferent, continuous in their passive dominance. The waves were thick and dark, a wary shade of deep blue. With no land in sight, I felt vulnerable. On a whim, the unrelenting fathoms could swallow us whole without so much as a pinch of effort. We were but a speck of potential flotsam, a vessel of crossed fingers bobbing in the jarring chop.

101

By Poseidon's grace we arrived on solid ground, my legs taking their time to adjust to their new-found stability. Lingering nausea kept me company as we took in the lay of the land. Already it was clear that this was a different sort of Japan. Sparsely populated, only a few thousand people called the sub-tropical island home. Having grown up in small-town Canada, I felt comfortable in the rural landscape. It was simple, unpolished. It was also decidedly not white. With only half a handful of Caucasian visitors at a time, Kumejima offered an interesting cultural role reversal. Here I was the minority. I stood out, my foreign privilege a visible shade of off-white. Growing up in a decidedly white town and having gone to a decidedly white university, this was a new experience — and a profound one. Privilege can be a subtle, invasive entity. It takes a lot of conscious effort to break though the filters and biases it imbues. It requires being critical of your own views and of the framework of your experience. In that regard, I've found travel — a privileged act in itself — to be a helpful tool and my visit to Kumejima was, at the very least, an illuminating personal milestone

As my stomach settled, we meandered up the coast with no real plans or direction, nor even a map of the little isle to guide us. The island itself was lined by sandy beaches, and where there weren't beaches there were lush sugar plantations as far as the eye could see. Most of the work, if not all of it, was done by hand. It was old school farm work, the kind that breaks backs in the most literal of ways. It stood in stark contrast to the visage of a hyper-modern Japan, a far cry from the sleepless streets of luminous Tokyo. Even when compared to the relatively tedious farm work I did back in Canada, this was something else entirely. Every so often we would pause on the beach to watch the farmers work. One would hack away at the sugar stalks as someone else collected the fallen canes and bundled them into piles. Even in the humid sub-tropical climate they worked in long-sleeve shirts, bandanas fastened around their necks to battle both the heat and the pooling sweat. Wide-brimmed conical hats were the norm, wrapped fastidiously around their heads as protection from the worst of the dog day sun. By no means did it seem to be a particularly easy job, but honest work rarely is. I suppose back breaking labour is, perhaps, a reasonable price to pay for paradise. Then again, I wasn't the one struggling out in the fields.

After standing distant witness to the laborious task we continued our clueless exploration, trudging up the beach simply because we could. We trekked down the coast for a few hours until, rather surprisingly, we discovered we had walked the length of the island. We arrived at what was either a small hotel or an apartment building...or possibly both. The unattractive concrete building was something of a visual stain; it was a rather drab addition to the vibrant landscape, yet it enabled us to maneuver away from the beach and onto our first road. Which was a problem.

For better or worse, roads inherently require you to make a choice: which direction will you go? We had nowhere in specific to go, no particular destination to arrive at. With us was a tent and enough food to last us a few days. All we needed was somewhere to camp. Tentatively paralyzed by indecision, we were at a loss. Shoulders slumped, I glanced one way, and then the other, squinting as if there was some secret clue that would reveal itself if I only looked harder. We hummed and hawed and then hummed some more, eventually deciding to leave our fate up to a coin toss.

That's when we met our guide.

A middle-aged Japanese man approached us in his van, rolling to a stop as we stood adrift at the side of the road. Now, this is precisely the kind of situation one usually tries to avoid when alone in a foreign place. The semi-tinted windows and the dozen rusted-out dents were far from reassuring, but we held our ground. After all, I had a bigger knife, this time

— a lesson learned from Costa Rica. It wouldn't be long, however, before I found out he had an even bigger one.

Leaning out the window, the potential murderer asked us where we were going. His choppy English was only slightly better than my abysmal Japanese, so it was understandable when he didn't comprehend my reply.

"Uhh…we don't know…?"

There was hardly a moment's pause before launched open the door and told us to get in. Admittedly, there was a slightly longer pause before we did.

As it turned out, the bespectacled man was an ice cream salesman. We would have appreciated this fact ever more so if my partner and I weren't vegans, but it seemed oddly fitting nevertheless. After piling onto the worn and sun-faded back seat, the sliding door was slammed behind us. The engine kicked to life and our new-found chauffeur started rolling down the semi-paved road. Not knowing what he was doing nor where we were going, we couldn't really protest. With a shrug and a smile, we buckled our seat belts and readied ourselves for an off-the-cuff adventure. So much for not getting into vans with strangers who offer you candy![19]

We headed inland toward the rolling hills that rose up from beyond the beach. Lining the winding road were rows of Japanese cherry trees, their knotted branches reaching out to cast frail shadows over the pavement. The delicate petals caught the sun and shone a cascading pink light throughout the dishevelled and run-down van. In the slight gusts of wind the flowers would tumble free, the road littered with windblown petals, soft under our bare feet as we stepped out of the van. We were standing in a graveyard of rarefied grace, inevitable and sacred ground. We worked to capture the fleeting beauty with a few photos, accepting that those photos would never truly capture their transitory elegance.

From there we drove to one of the many sugar plantations that called Kumejima home. Our guide chatted up a farmer who was working by the road, no doubt explaining that he caught two clueless *gaijin* and was giving us the unofficial tour.[20] After shooting the shit, he meandered back toward the van where we were sitting, the two of us still not quite sure what was happening. Pulling open the side door, his thick hands reached under my seat to pull out a *kama* — a small, sharp sickle. I froze, momentarily tense. The bitter taste of fight or flight crawled up my throat like reverse vomit. In North America, when you are in a stranger's van and he pulls a weapon on you, you're fucked. That isn't the case in Japan, however.

Smiling, no doubt clueless to the terror he had instilled, our guide marched back over to the farm, climbed over a fence, and bent down to cut a few stalks of sugarcane. Handing each of us an oozing chunk, he gestured that we should give them a try. Grabbing a foot-long cane, I gave it a chew. It was warm and sweet, but tough and fibrous. I chomped the stalk to bits while we continued down the narrow road, slurping every drop from the syrupy stalk. Liquid gold.

Eventually we came to a tiny cafe where we once again paused. Our guide, going above and beyond our wildest expectations, bought us each a coffee. We sat in the quaint little shop while he talked up the server, leaving us to our own conversation which predominately focused on just how wonderful this person was. Now, I must confess that I hate coffee. It's a gross acquired taste that I have never bothered to waste my time nor money acquiring. Out of sheer respect and appreciation for his assistance, however, I downed that black cup of Japanese joe. That kind of charity and goodwill is something I have experienced quite a bit on the road, perhaps even more so than when at home. And I am not the only traveller who has experienced it. There is something about helping a stranger that resonates with people from all walks of life and has led to some wonderfully serendipitous moments...and you don't get much more serendipitous than a guided tour by an ice-cream salesman on a backwater island in Japan. I'll drink a gross coffee to that any day of the week.

Our final stop was a campground where we said farewell to our impromptu guide. I will never see that man again — I never even got his name — and yet here I sit, many a year later, reflecting on his profound kindness. I've done my best to pay it forward, and I will certainly continue to do so because it's these simple joys and kind gestures that make a place noteworthy, regardless of what relics lay amongst the history.

~~~~~

Our unanticipated ice cream truck adventure was not our only run in with generous strangers in Okinawa. Back on the main island, we couldn't resist sticking out our thumbs in Naha, the laid-back capital city. Hardly veteran hitchhikers, we nevertheless thought to test the limits of our good fortune. We had heard through the hostel grapevine that Japanese drivers love to pick up foreign hitchhikers as it gives them a chance to test their English and sneak a cross-cultural peek. With our eyes set on making it to the tip of the island, hitchhiking seemed like a worthwhile endeavour. We parked ourselves on the curb, primed our smiles and patience, and waited for someone's curiosity to get the better of them.

It only took five minutes.

An American ex-pat was the first to pick us up. We climbed into his two-door hatchback, offering up a heartfelt thanks before we started with the necessary introductions. Wading into the small talk, it didn't take long for our generous driver to open up about why he was in Japan: he was a wanted criminal in the US.

Sigh.

Having fled the country after paying his bond, he jumped a plane to Okinawa and took up island life. Naturally, he didn't look back. I didn't think it appropriate to ask precisely what his crime was, though I crossed my fingers it wasn't for murdering hitchhikers. He was the talkative type, grateful for an opportunity to engage some other *gaijin* — *gaijin* who weren't American soldiers — in some small talk. Since the end of WWII, the majority of westerners on the island have been American soldiers, a social group he wasn't keen to interact with.

While his distaste for the US army was palpable, his love for Japan was tremendous. To him, he had stumbled into a paradise, with specific admiration for the weather, the food, and the women. As he weaved toward the outskirts of the city he went into greater detail about his favourite aspect.

"Now, of course I'm married — you have to be in Japan."

He flashed his wedding band, reaching over to show me the gold ring as he turned down a side street to where he would drop us off...or murder us.

"But I have a few girlfriends, too. Japanese girls love westerners, dude. You would find a girl here *like that* — probably even a bunch, man!"

He seemed to keep forgetting that my partner was sitting right beside me, and she wasn't entirely keen on his suggestion that I drop everything and take up a new life in paradise. Side-stepping his casual sexist and derogatory comments, I thanked him for the ride. It turns out he was a lover, not a murderer, so we clambered out of the vehicle unscathed. As we headed back toward the sidewalk of the main road he gave us a wave, shouting his final goodbye:

"Don't forget what I said, man! They LOVE it!"

Looking to my girlfriend, I offered up an awkward, wincing

smile.

"Maybe we should stay longer..."

Before I could finish the sentence, she had already hammered her fist into my arm.

It was only ten minutes of waiting before our next ride arrived. A young Japanese man who worked for Coca-Cola pulled over and waved us into his work truck. We traded stumbling introductions in each other's language as best we could, laughing at our mutual linguistic shortcomings. Pointing to a map, we conveyed that we were going all the way to the tip of the island, just over one-hundred kilometres away. He was shocked, a slight flush coming to his face which soon transformed into an uncomfortable silence. He wasn't going that far, no doubt because he was actually on shift...which, for us, was perfectly fine. We were hitchhiking and would take what we could get with smile. Beggars, after all, cannot be choosers. We presumed he felt pressured to take us all the way and attempted to clarify otherwise. He nevertheless took us much further than he planned, dropping us off with a couple bottles of ice-cold Coke before doing a U-turn and driving back to wherever he was heading before his cross-cultural detour.

Sitting in the shade to sip our farewell drinks, we couldn't help but wonder how these people would interpret our exchanges. How would they remember us? Would the young Coke delivery boy talk to us with his colleagues? Would we be brought up at dinner as an interesting aside? On a deeper level, we wondered why they would pick us up to begin with. What is about someone that prods them to take that risk, to slow down for a stranger and let them into their vehicle — their life — if only for a short while? It was amusing to reflect upon as we waited, thumbs out to entice each passing car, that our entire adventure was merely a "By the way..." or "Funny story..." to those we had encountered so far.

By the time the next car stopped for us our drinks were long empty and our bladders well full. With no initial luck, we had moseyed up the highway for the better part of a sweaty hour, our backs and brows a slippery mess. When a car rolled to a stop in front of us we noticed that there were already four people crammed into its crowded confines. Japanese cars, after all, are not known for their spaciousness.

Three generations of Japanese women greeted us through the open window and waved us into their automotive sardine can. Being the tallest, I saddled into the front seat, taking the smallest kid on my lap. My partner shuffled into the hump seat, wedged between the grandma and the 12-year-old who acted as our translator. Once more we dove into a round of small-talk, asking and answering questions about families, jobs, homes, and life in our respected countries. And our names.

"Watashiwa Chris desu." (My name is Chris.)

I gave a partial to the bow to the family, after which they applauded, astonished that I managed the most basic of greeting.

"Hello Kurusu! Nicea tu meet you!"

Gesturing to my co-adventurer Lauren, I continued.

"Ano...korewa Lauren desu." (This is Lauren.)

The grandmother replied first, tenderly patting Lauren on the shoulder, nodding her head in understanding.

"Ahhh Boren. Hajimeimashite!" (Please to meet you!)

"No no, sorry. It's Lauren. Laur--"

"Ahh ok, ok! Bōren, yes!"

Once more red in the face, Lauren worked to correct their

pronunciation but I cut her off, already grinning as I patted her on the knee.

"Hai. Boren. Korewa Boren-desu"

The family all chimed in, repeating her name: Boren.

They each went and shared their names with us, repeating them slowly so we could comprehend the syllables. After completing the name game, they offered us more applause before diving into deeper questions about our lives outside Japan. What do you do? Are you married? Do you have children? Does it snow where you live? Have you been to Tokyo? Can you drive a car? Their curiosity was boundless and honest, and we laughed away a few dozen kilometres before coming to a stop in Nago. Before letting us return to our vagabond ways the mother graciously bought us lunch, a traditional Japanese meal known as "the hamburger."

We didn't feel it appropriate to turn down their heartwarming gesture, nor did we have the linguistic ability to do so, so we sneakily picked away the meat and ate the buns and toppings. We slid the patties back into the wrapper without anyone noticing, thanking them repeatedly for their hospitality. To this day, whenever I get caught up in how shitty human beings can be I remember that family. Their kindness, their openness, serves a permanent reminder that wonderful people are out there. It's a refreshing thought to fall back upon.

Also, Boren.

They dropped us off on the outskirts of Nago, a small city with a curious tourist trap: Pineapple Park. We couldn't resist a visit to the cheesy theme park (no doubt designed for children) where we rode pineapple rides, bought cheap pineapple souvenirs, and ate as much pineapple as our taste buds could handle. And then some. I ate free samples until my tongue bled, the sweet acidic bristles cutting my mouth to shreds. What can I say, when things are free I sometimes get carried away.

The park itself, in true Japanese fashion, was absurd and nonsensical, a fun change of pace from our thumbs-out explorations. In the grand tradition of pretty much all my travels, however, I struggled to find our accommodation after our play date was over. We knew the hostel was on the coast somewhere as it was a laid-back surf shack...but on an island the size of Okinawa that isn't very helpful information. While walking around the supposed vicinity we were offered assistance by an older Japanese man. Once again, it was a guy with a van. Instead of ice cream he offered us some oranges and reassured us in broken English that he knew where we were going. I had a tinge of suspicion in my gut, but we had been lucky so far so I brushed it off and jumped into the vehicle.

I should have listened to my gut.

Within minutes we realized that he was driving the wrong direction, heading back out of the city. We tried to convey that it was the wrong direction but he didn't seem to understand and declined our suggestion to stop. A little bit of worry started to blossom in my chest, and after ten minutes of weaving through traffic toward the highway we told him to just pull over. He was rather confused, but the situation didn't feel right. I may be dumb enough to eat pineapple until I bleed, but I trust my intuition. We quickly thanked him for the ride and the oranges and bolted, once more stuck on the highway.

Shuffling back from whence we came, slightly annoyed but happy to be out of the van, we approached a young couple and asked them for directions. The husband was sure he knew precisely where the hostel was, so he offered us a ride for the final few kilometres. We slide into the backseat beside their sleeping infant who was strapped into a bulky car seat. Inching along the coast, it became clear that even our new hosts couldn't find the hidden abode. We ended up spending 25 minutes searching the coastline and nearby suburbs, snacking on children's digestive cookies as we peered out the window for any signs of backpackerness. On a few occasions the couple stopped to ask directions from convenience store staff, leaving us with their running vehicle AND their baby. If that isn't trust, I don't know what is.

In the end, we found the hostel tucked away on a quiet, empty beach. It was about as stereotypically chill as you can get: hammocks hung every which way, surfboards were littered in the sand, and there were no locks on any of the doors. Graffitied greetings were scribbled on every surface, in languages from every corner of the world. With the city in the distance, we were left to linger in the soft gurgling of capping waves, in the subtle smells of distant fish and not-so-distant wetsuits. Lights from the highway were blurred and flyspeck, a lifetime away. Curled up in our wooden bunks, we were the only two backpackers there. With a faded black marker, I scribbled a few words on the bed frame. It was proof to the world that I had made it; proof that there were still good, kind people out there.

It was — and is — an important reminder.

Cheque, Please

A Lesson in Financial Vigilance

I used to travel with my cheque book. Not the once-widely-accepted traveller's cheques but standard, plain personal cheques. This was in 2009, when cheques were already a dying form of financial transaction. For some reason, I believed they could come in handy during an emergency abroad, say, if I lost my wallet. I figured, should something unfortunate occur I would at least have access to my money in the interim via these watermarked and antiquated documents. Day after day they sat in my bag, rolled up into a hidden compartment, ever at the ready; a folded bundle of semi-embarrassment. I would check on them — no pun intended — daily, making sure that they didn't get left behind or disintegrate into the ether of days gone by. They stuck with me, stubborn relics that they were, until one day — the only day — when I needed to use them overseas. Call it an emergency transaction.

After getting established at the seaside campground where the Ice Cream Man left us, we decided to head out and explore some more of the island — this time on foot. We had heard from some locals that there were a few hiking trails around, and one particular place of interest: Mefuga, aka Vagina Rock. Looming at the edge of the island, Mefuga was a sizeable vagina-shaped cliff considered to be a symbol of fertility. Many women and couples would visit the...uh, vag rock, when they were having trouble getting pregnant. When we arrived, having spent the morning crossing the entirety of the isle on foot, we saw a few people there, no doubt asking the towering vag for a helping hand.

To recover from our hike, we picnicked in the vaginal shadow of Mefuga. Sprawled against the rocks, the salty breeze lapped cooling gusts of wind along our exhausted and sweaty forms. Somewhere beyond the horizon was China, though no amount of squinting into the distance brought it into view. In our immediate vicinity, against the timeless azure backdrop of the Pacific, we were faced with a much more shocking panorama: all along the coast, garbage had washed ashore. And not just a few stray items, but a monumental sum of debris. Plastic bags, shards of containers and wood, hunks of metal — the coastline was littered with it all. Wedged between the base of the cliff were heaps of trash, the cultural aftermath from nearby China and mainland Japan. With every capped wave, the junk piles rolled further onto land, smothering the exposed coastline. We sat there, tragic witnesses to the hidden cost of modern day life. If there is anything we humans are good at, it's ruining beautiful things.

Having properly paid homage to the towering stone sex organ, we trudged back to camp. It was, to say the least, a taxing endeavour. More than the distance, it was the humidity that was our formidable foe. We leaked salty stains all across the island, introducing the locals to our alien pit funk as we wafted our stench beyond the trails and into town. With only a few kilometers left to crush, my partner "Boren" started to feel ill.[21] I was exhausted but in good spirits, so I chalked it up to her just being unfit. She parked herself on a bench, grumpily insisting that we hail a cab. We couldn't have been more than an hour from our campsite, so I put up a fuss. I'm painfully cheap...err, frugal, but eventually caved to her iron insistence.

The cabbie dropped us off at a grocery store where we could restock our water, grab a few things for dinner, and bask in the enlivening but morally-questionable AC. I devoured a block of fried tofu while Boren half-collapsed in the shade. I let her recover, content to rest my legs and stare at all the locals as they shopped and went about their regular lives. When it was time to head to camp she didn't even make it ten feet. Stumbling over to a storm drain, she bent to a knee and puked. For a small girl, she managed to hack up quite a display. Retching up the remnants of lunch, she covered the entire storm drain in bile, an appalling off-white gut stew. As she spat up unidentifiable chunks, an exceedingly-aged woman hobbled by. Stooped by her years, she was old as time itself, her skin so weathered and wrinkled you could have washed your laundry in its creases. Looking down at Boren, she shook her head with a *tsk*, chuckling at the avoidable misfortune. I couldn't help but smile as well.

Smiles aside, heat stroke is a serious concern and I now had to help my partner recover from her dehydration and exhaustion. I had water to lend, but nothing to help with the...mess. No paper towel or Kleenex, and I wasn't willing to sacrifice my favourite bandana. I searched my bag for anything that could help her, finding only my long-since-abandoned cheque book.

I tore off a cheque, voided it, and handed it to her so she could wipe the vomit clean from her mouth and hands. She did, resting her hand against the fence as she caught her breath. And then she glared at me, pausing for effect before she yelled.

"You voided it!?"

"Yeah, I voided it. You can never be too careful, right?"

Christopher Kevin Oldfield

Connecticut Blowjobs

A Lesson in Living Boldly

"So, would you like a blowjob?"

Fuck. I should have seen this coming.

I could feel my stomach sink, seeking refuge from the conversational shrapnel that exploded into the vehicle. Awkward pricks of panic danced along my jawline as it tightened. There would be no airbag for this crash.

"Uhhhhhhhh…"

It dragged on like the empty highway before us.

"Um. Thanks. For the offer? Uhh…but I'm good."

I trailed off, my voice ticking up a few octaves as my brain derailed. A silent, dragging moment began to form between us, hoovering in the cramped space that was my mother's two-door car. The sweatiness of my palms became vastly apparent as my mind recovered from the chit-chat sideswipe. What else could I do but smile and ramble?

"Thanks, though. Really."

She shrugged a careless shrug, her shoulders barely rising.

"Ok."

She might as well have been filing her nails as she talked,

boldly indifferent to the awkward exchange. Curled up into the passenger seat of my borrowed car, she radiated nonchalance about the whole affair, as if she had just casually offered me a stick of gum. Her voice was quiet and soft, the kind of voice you need to really listen to in order to make out the muted sounds. But it was confident. Experienced. For better or worse, this was a conversation she was familiar with.

I kept my eyes locked ahead, focusing on the yellow lines that blurred the highway before me. Admittedly, I was at a loss for how to continue the conversation.

So I laughed and prayed she didn't hear me.

I was on my way to Connecticut, for no other reason than to drive from Canada to the ocean. I picked the shore of that great state as my final destination because…well, to be honest, there was no rational reason. I just looked at the map, picked a state, and drove. With half a dozen freshly burned CD's and a longing for adventure, I hit the open road.

Or, perhaps more accurately, the open road hit me.

In response to something of an existential crisis, I jumped headlong at the chance to escape the clutches of work and school and a relationship. I needed a new perspective on things, some time to collect the scattered parts of myself and cobble it all back together. Call it a quarter life crisis. One of several.

With access to a vehicle, and with America at my doorstep, it seemed fitting to venture south to see what adventures were afoot.

There weren't many. Probably because I went to Connecticut. The Nutmeg State.

But there was one.

As I rolled away from a generic truck stop on my way south, I saw someone standing on the curb. Being on an adventure — and without thinking — I took my foot off the gas and rolled over to the dusty shoulder. From the haphazard glance I stole as I passed, my new-found passenger looked to be a scrawny teenager of punk-ish association. I figured it was just some social outcast looking to escape the confines of the Nowheresville which we both found ourselves in. Having roots in the punk scene myself, back when my hair was long (and when, to be honest, I had hair) and my music was loud, I thought I would pay it forward and pick up this roadside hobo.

Dressed in varying shades of faded black, I watched as they slung their torn rucksack into my back seat. The smell hit me first. The stale odour of sweat and piss, of an unwashed body wearing unwashed clothes percolated into the car, tickling my nostrils. It was an eye-watering stench, feral and unforgiving. But this was the Road, this was adventure. I shrugged it off with a quick drop of the window, greeting my new co-pilot as he rolled into the seat.

Turns out, however, he was a she.

The scrawny vagabond was actually a middle-aged woman, a pale and freckled ginger with quiet eyes half-hidden by a tangled mess of scrappy hair. Her meagre frame was hard pressed to top 100lbs, and I was honestly rather shocked she could toss her hefty backpack around the way she did. It was that hidden strength, that familiarity, that betrayed her nomadic lifestyle. This was not her first rodeo.

She slid breezily into the car, barely dispersing the air as she locked herself into the seat. Her smile was measured, but genuine. A testing of the water. Her eyes darted up from under the shadow of a black hoodie to meet mine.

"Hello."

Her tone said it all. This was both a greeting and a thank you, a soft welcome and desperate thanks, all wrapped up into a single, delicate introduction. She radiated simplicity, so much so that I was put off at first. There was no veneer, no velvet over iron. She didn't put on a face or attitude to make pleasantries or seem more likeable than she was. She just was. There was a rawness to her being, to the way she sat, the way she talked. Like she had seen it all and was still processing. Still recovering.

I politely prodded her with questions, curious as to what series of events brought us together. She laid out her story in bits and pieces, painting a fragmented portrait of a full-time nomad and hitchhiker. Living on the curb, relying on others to get from A to B, my nameless co-pilot was often thrust into uncomfortable situations. While many drivers were happy to help another human being out, there were plenty — a disgusting amount, I'd say — who expected something in return.

Cue the offer of a bj.

She painted a vivid picture of life on the road, the less-than-glamorous narrative you won't see on Instagram or Facebook. And while she claimed she was perfectly okay sucking a dick in exchange for a few hundred miles I couldn't help but wonder if that was her genuine view. But maybe that's just because I wouldn't want a dick in my mouth, regardless of the mileage.

What ever happened to just helping people out? To seeing someone in need and saying, "Sure, I can do something." If it's no skin off your back, what's the big deal? Call me old fashioned, but if you coerce someone into sucking your dick for a ride, you're a piece of shit. But maybe I'm just naive.

I guided the conversation back to travel and we talked about our mutual adventures. She had thumbed her way around

Canada and the US, darting as far as Central America over the years. She left her family — her husband and kids — back home in British Colombia because she wasn't happy. One day, she just packed up, said goodbye, and sold her soul to the Road. She hadn't been back since, bouncing around here and there with no real goal or objective. It was a bold life, to say the very least. There was a temptation there, I confess. Being neck-deep in a life I wasn't loving, the thought of packing up and hitting the road had its charms. But I wasn't that bold. And I certainly wasn't ready for that much dick in my face.

I don't remember where I dropped her off precisely, but I remember it was raining. Grey skies wept fat drops onto the windshield, our farewell set to the tune of pouring rain on metal and glass. The last time I saw her, she was shuffling through the downpour toward a big rig parked at a Husky station. Shouldering her bag, she waved goodbye, her face radiating indifference to the grey and swift droplets that battered the cement around her. I wouldn't have been surprised if she stayed dry.

~~~~~

The next night I found myself at, of all places, a TGI Fridays. *So this is what my life has come to.* To be honest, I'd never been to one and this was America after all. Call it a cultural exploration. Why the fuck a vegan who doesn't drink would even bother to go to one is beyond me. I suppose it could have been worse. I could have went to an Applebee's.

Nestled in a spacious booth below a muted TV playing sports highlights, I rifled through the menu for some vegan offerings. When the waiter finally strolled over, I placed my order.

"Can I have the sweet potato fries, but with BBQ sauce instead of the aioli?"

Wearing the light-hearted mask of all service staff, he replied.

"Bold choice, sir. It'll be right up"

That's What You Get for Waking Up in...Vilnius?

A Lesson in Conflict Resolution

Hostel life isn't for everyone. The creaking bunks, comings and goings at all hours, and crowded confines are hardly conducive to a healthy and well-rested lifestyle. Toss in the occasional douchebag who listens to music without headphones or turns the lights on at 2 a.m., and you've got yourself a recipe for an anxiety attack.

What hostels lack in privacy they usually make up for in atmosphere, the forced close-quarter interactions spurring on friendships and adventures and ill-conceived sex romps in semi-public places. Top it all off with a price that appeases an empty wallet and you've got yourself a place to crash.

I've been an avid lover of hostels since I started traveling, though I confess that love has faded over the years, morphing into more of a tolerance than anything else. We've had some good times, to be sure, but after so long together we're starting to drift apart. The raucous late nights have lost their charm, replaced by an appreciation of early, productive mornings. Every now and then? Sure, I'll spice up my life and fall into my old, nostalgic habits. But it can't last. We will never split, of course — we're too set in our ways for that — so we'll go on in shared tolerance of one another, hoping things get better but knowing it's an uphill battle.

For ten bucks a night, though, I'll happily tolerate that battle.

~~~~~

It sounded like someone fell from their bunk.

It was just shy of 6 a.m. and I was already awake, grazing on social media updates from the comfort of my bottom bunk. What cacophonous snoring there was — and Lord knows, there was plenty — had died down to little more than sporadic snorts and gurgles, a sign that morning was almost upon my fellow backpackers.

That's when I heard the thud.

I felt it, too. The wooden floor shook, rattling my creaky, curtained dormitory refuge. Peeking around the damp, neon green travel towel that provided me with privacy, I glanced a pair of tanned feet firmly planted on the floor. I followed them upward, eyes adjusting to take in the hairy legs and checkered boxer shorts that were propped against the three-step ladder.

Nobody had fallen. Someone just didn't know how to use their tippy-toes.

The rest of the dorm's inhabitants were still fast asleep. There was a ritual pub crawl the previous night, and most of my roommates had taken part. They kicked the night off with some shots of Lithuanian moonshine — we were in Vilnius, after all — and I'm sure things went downhill from there. Fortunately, I dodged those boozy bullets by staying in and catching up on some work. So much for #yolo.

Within a few seconds of the mini quake, I heard the familiar sound of liquid spilling. It was loud, no doubt pouring from the top of the bunk. Maybe an open water bottle, or perhaps the remnants of a spilled beer. After a few seconds, though, it didn't stop.

It wasn't, I realized, a spilled container.

It was the guy.

He was pissing.

(On someone's backpack and belongings I later discovered)

For whatever reason, I didn't lunge into action. From my perspective, it just looked like he was pissing on the floor and I wasn't keen to interrupt a half-sleeping/half-drunk Indian man's early morning routine...likely because I would have ended up in the splash zone.

The Spaniard, whose bed he was pissing beside, however, was not so keen to let things slide. The stout Spanish backpacker awoke with understandable confusion.

"What the fuck?!"

He ripped his blankets off, shouting at the Indian man who still hadn't really moved or reacted. He just stood there in a piss coma, oblivious to it all.

Until he got drilled in the face with a solid right hook. Naturally, that woke him the fuck up.

The slap-crunch of fist-to-face is such a distinct sound. It doesn't really sound like a punch on TV or in the movies...it has a much more unpolished ring. It's a visceral sound, one you can almost feel. I grimaced as I heard it. *Maybe I should have said something sooner...*

The punch, which was followed by raised voices, woke the rest of the dorm room up. The Spanish backpacker shoved his urinating foe into the ladder, grabbing him by the scruff of his pastel t-shirt, yelling and cursing in a mix of English and Spanish.

Hands up, spewing apologies, the clueless pisser was just

coming around to what was happening. And boy was he embarrassed. He flailed, but didn't fight back as the Spaniard attacked.

Fortunately, he had stopped pissing. The scuffle didn't last long.

The rest of us intervened, our brains puttering into motion as we jumped from our bunks to make sure no more punches were thrown. Pulling the two apart, we defused the piss-soaked situation before things blew up even more. A rambling apology gushed from the Indian man as he grabbed a roll of paper and started dabbing up the pool of piss at his feet. His head was low, his face framed with equal parts shame and confusion

Unsure of sure how to react, we all just sort of waited. After all, it isn't every day someone pisses on someone else and a fight breaks out.

At least, not where I come from.

Using his feet and some one-ply paper towel, he lazily mopped up the various puddles, shuffling the papers around his feet until they were saturated. Bits of piss-soaked paper were left around the floor, tiny shreds catching and tearing on the uneven floor boards. I heard an exasperated sigh exhale from the petite Swede who bunked above me, her head collapsing back down to her pillow. Her curtain shot closed once more, cutting her off from the scene. And the scent.

Warm, pissy air wafted through the room as the sun trickled in from a half-covered window. Were this a luxury resort, I'd be waking up to the smell of room service, to the invigorating aroma of strong coffee, the sweet invitation of waffles or pancakes drenched in real maple syrup…

But this was no luxury resort.

I fumbled into my flip flops with a chuckle, careful to avoid the remaining puddles, and plodded to the bathroom for my morning piss. Being extra careful, however, I decided to sit down and pee. After all, nobody likes a pissy floor.

Christopher Kevin Oldfield

The Russia Chronicles

A Few Lessons in *уважение*

One needs people, even if it's only to have someone to swear at.
~ Bazarov, from Ivan Turgenev's *Fathers and Sons*

Superman/Red Son

Moscow in October was a grim sight. I watched the grey city ebb and flow in tandem with the swirling concrete-coloured clouds that hung low above the Motherland, subtly dispiriting. A ray of sunshine would work wonders here, and I made a mental note to Google the summer weather averages for Russia. I could already smell the coming rain in the city air as I exited our hostel, a building so tucked away down a back alley that we spent an hour trying to find it the night prior. Wandering Moscow at midnight was something I had hoped to avoid, as every single person who gave me travel advice for Russia had, in fact, been robbed during their visit. In a country with such visible economic inequality, I was hardly surprised. I had already seen cars older than I was being driven side-by-side with polished Hummers and flashy limousines. Moreover, I was keenly aware that I stood out. While not exactly shunned, Moscow felt unwelcoming; the city stood in stereotypical stoic indifference to my existence. I was already starting to empathize with Dostoevsky.

Before the rain hit, we made our way to the subway and trudged down the endless stairs into the hidden subterranean corridors of the capital. Where in North America you might find convenience stores selling gum and Red Bull, we passed stalls selling underwear and lingerie, a pharmacy, and a guy selling all sorts of knives and weapons. Everything one might need for their daily commute.

After browsing the blades, we rode a series of escalators so far underground that the city above could have been levelled into oblivion right then and there and we wouldn't have heard or felt a thing — which I think was the point. The air that far below the surface wasn't quite stale, but the fresh smell of rain was now long gone, lost in the cavernous confines of the semi-modern underground.

We hopped on an old but well-maintained subway car and creaked our way across the once-soviet city toward the train station. The car was sparsely populated, with half a handful of folks littered about in typical subway fashion. To my immediate left was a business-y man of middle age, deftly standing and reading a Russian newspaper as we sped along. Directly across from me sat two hooligan types sporting the stereotypical baggy clothing and dangling chains one might find in a tacky music video from the early 90's. They were looking at me and my partner, who was sitting at my side, the way a shark might look at a surfboard: with curious potential. We had our giant packs in front of us, the hefty bags stuffed and brimming as they rested on the floor, pinned between our knees. Our trip had taken us from Belgium to France to Germany to Latvia, and now to Moscow. It would take the two of us further still, through Russia, Mongolia, China, and Hong Kong. The crossing of these multiple climates had forced our hand when it came to packing and our 60L bags sat heavy. Resting them upon the subway floor was an appreciated reprieve for our weary shoulders.

It was then, when I was lost in thought and inquisitive observation, that the hooligan teens spoke up. With a thick accent, one of them pointed to my bag.

"Haw machh did you pay forr dhat bag?"

It was precisely the kind of question one hopes to avoid in a new country, especially when asked by someone who could likely kick the foreign shit out of you. It was *especially* not the kind of question I wanted to be answering when I remembered that there were several — yes, more than one — stores selling knives within the underground shopping area. Granted, there were also several shops selling tacky women's underwear but that fact really wasn't on my mind at the moment. Knife stores, it seemed, were like the Starbucks of Russia, and the chance that one of these curious individuals had themselves a razor-sharp, venti-sized blade seemed relatively high. I responded the only way I could think of: I smiled politely.

He asked again, this time more assertively. I mumbled a half-hearted answer about not knowing precisely.

"The price? Oh. Uh…I don't know. I used a gift card, I think…and it was on sale? So…"

I let my words hang with a shrug and a smile. He didn't quite appreciate, nor comprehend, my rambling response. Shifting in his seat to talk with his companion, he then fired some follow-up questions in a mix of Russian and English in hopes of getting a rise out of us. It was clear they wanted to make us uncomfortable. They were doing a relatively good job.

It was also clear that we were becoming noticeably ill at ease as they started to reach over to our bags. I kept up a firm wall of Canadian politeness to deflect as much awkward and discomfort as I could, but it was a losing battle. Fortunately for us, our own private Red Son was there to save us from anything worse than a mere harassing.[22] The business man, who memory depicts as a Russian doppelganger of Francois Hollande, set his paper down on the empty seat beside me. He stepped in front of us to confront the bullies, adjusting his spectacles to get a good look at the teens. Briefcase in hand, he completely interrupted their verbal strides with his firm, parental tone. He wasn't overly aggressive but candidly told them to piss off...or whatever the equivalent Russian phrase is. After exchanging some semi-heated words with our hero, they gave up on their fruitless efforts of harassing us. Our Comrade of Steel nevertheless remained vigilant, unflinching in his protection of us until the kids decided we were no longer worth their effort and got off the train. I shook his hand, mumbling a series of thanks before we, too, left the subway car to continue on our way across the Grand Duchy of Moscow.

Looking back, I saw our hero pick up his paper, adjust his glasses once more, and return to reading. I can't help but wonder if he remembers that incident, 6 years later. I remember it so vividly because it was one of the first 'uncomfortable situations' I found myself in abroad. When you're confronted like that, even mildly, as we were, it really hits home the fact that you are in a foreign land, *you don't belong*. Class and privilege come swirling in like a social sucker punch, preying on the uninitiated. Chances are that when it happens — and it will, if you travel enough — you'll be alone. Because even Superman can't be everywhere.

The Hounds of Lake Baikal

"Just stick your head in!"

I'm shouting into the brisk wind, cupping my mouth with one hand as the other holds a camera. My partner Christine has lost a bet — one of several, in fact — and has quite reluctantly trudged herself into the icy waters of Lake Baikal. It's October, and the water is far from temperate.

I'm on the shore, shivering in a makeshift bathing suit as I verbally prod her into paying her debt. Understandably, she's hesitating. The 12 megapixel "adventure camera" is allegedly waterproof so I step out into the dark waves, my teeth already chattering. At 150lbs (likely less, after being on the road for a few weeks) I hardly have the fat reserves to stave off the autumn chill of Siberia. I can feel my blood congealing as it pumps from my feet upward, my skin edging on a shade pale-blue. I'm not designed for cold.

Fuck it.

I charge forward into the deathwater. I don't know if I'm shouting but I feel like I am, gritting my teeth as the adrenaline catches up with my dash. I plunge into the frigid shallows of the deepest lake in the world, submerging myself for but the merest pinch of a second. I can't say for certain, but I'm convinced my heart has stopped, frozen mid-beat as it sinks below the surface. My legs press into the rocky muck and coil, rocketing me from Poseidon's watery grasp. By the time my eyes re-focus I'm already springing back to shore, retinas locked on the towel I haphazardly tossed on the stony beach. My nipples have never been harder, my testicles never smaller. I hope the damage isn't permanent.

Wrapped in a towel, the world slips away. I cannot describe the invigorating feeling of being *slightly* less cold. It is miraculously sensational, even spiritual. The absence of pain truly is the best of comforts. I don't bother to wait for Christine, shimmying my way back to our cabin as she catches up. I cock my head sideways, shoulders high and tight, every muscle in my body spasming in refreshing protest. I clutch my towel with white-knuckle desperation, glancing back to Christine. Her hair isn't even wet.

So much for losing a bet.

We are in the village of Listvyanka and it's well into autumn. The hills that engulf us are already dotted with patches of dirty snow. Faint wisps of winter outline the trails up the slopes, visible only if you squint. Aside from the main paved road that leads into the semi-abandoned village, the rest of the lanes are a mess of mud. The path to our guesthouse is more pothole than road, more puddle than dry land. For months, the days have been getting darker, colder. Overcast and grey are the Russian colours we've become accustomed to. It's perfect sweater weather, albeit when it isn't pissing Russian rain.

We're staying in a quaint cabin along the coast at a guesthouse owned and operated by a lovely Russian woman. She speaks but a peppering of English and her name slips by in a cacophony of heavily-accented introductions. She is enthusiastic about everything — regardless of her level of actual comprehension — and her whirlwind presence adds an extra layer of eccentric coziness to the entire household. After our stopovers in the urban hubs of Moscow and Yekaterinburg, we've set aside a few days to escape into the wild. Already we feel more connected: to the land, the people, the culture. I'm a small-town kid at heart, and the familiar backdrop of forests and hills and open water invites me to let down my guard. It's a taste of home, the familiar wrapped in different robes.

Our room, like the house itself and most of the village, is crafted entirely from wood. It's one of Russia's prominent resources, and I can understand the draw (it's affordable!). Maybe it's...pine? I have no idea, but every room shares the polished texture and soft-white hue. Sporadic dark circles dress the walls like polka dot wallpaper, the knots adding texture to the backdrop. The entire cabin almost glows in the faint light, winning us over with its rustic charm. After a few days on a train, the extra space and warmth is a godsend, though having two single beds is hardly ideal. For now, though, I couldn't care less. Staring up at the mesmerizing planks above my bed, I am certain I can smell the forest. But maybe that is just a symptom of hypothermia.

We had hustled back toward the house after our morning plunge, half-naked and shivering blue. Crossing the main road into town, we were met with applause by some of the locals who had witnessed our daredevil antics in the frosty expanse. Maybe they were saluting us because they do this regularly and were proud to see some tourists doing the same. Then again, maybe they just thought we were idiots (a fistful of rubles says it was the latter).

When we finally made it back to our cabin our host was in stitches. It was a welcoming mix of both laughter and shock (a feeling I could relate to) but she nevertheless ushered us into our room, disappearing to hastily fetch more towels. Still shivering, I watch the video of our "swim" a few dozen times on my camera. I don't want to forget that moment — *this moment*. I close my eyes as my body strives to reheat itself, remembering the colours of the sky and water, the subtle shades of each. Gentle tufts of overcast clouds. Dark water, softly lapping the rugged shore. I ingrain it all into my memory. The uneven pebbles pressing up into my sandals. The icy tendrils splashing up my chest as I spring into the knee-deep waves. The piercing shock. The mud on my feet as we shuffle home through snow-melt puddles. The laughter. The knotted ceiling planks I'm looking at at this very moment as I lay here wrapped in a towel and two heavy blankets. I tattoo it onto my brain so that, in however many years, I can look back and say *I was here*. I want to keep this spark kindled for the rest of my life. In the dark and confusing times inevitably to come, when I'm lost and need to be reminded of warmth and light — of the burning fires that make me who I am — I will have this spark. When life exacts its heavy toll, I can look into the mirror and remind myself that I've tasted the cutting waters of Siberia. I've left muddy footprints in Irkutsk. I've pissed in the poorly-plumbed toilets a world away. Keep your shitty inspirational quotes, I'm carrying my own fire.

Lost in the lines of my ceiling, I relive the morning's icy swim and the past days and weeks of wandering Europe and Russia. My toes are regaining feeling, though I don't pay them much heed for my nose has just picked up a very distinct, and unfortunately familiar, aroma. It's a smell familiar to anyone with old-fashioned grandparents or lazy babysitters. It's the ever-fragrant redneck cologne: boiled hotdogs.

In addition to a comfy bed and a happy host, we are also served a complimentary breakfast every day. Buns, yogurt, eggs, cheese, and "sausage" (aka the aforementioned boiled hot dog) are all included in the modest price for our room. Granted, there isn't much here for a vegan to enjoy but that can really be said for the whole of Mother Russia. Christine, as a vegetarian, is able to make do where I can't, salvaging a semi-respectable meal from the morning offerings. After initially trying to explain that we both don't want the sausage, gesturing and Googling makeshift translations, we give up. In the confusion, our amiable innkeeper somehow concludes that, while I don't want any meat, Christine still does. And so, each day she dutifully boils one up for her, chatting away in indecipherable Russian as we rub the sleep from our tired eyes. While I ease in to stuffing my face with white bread and jam, Christine has the yogurt, cheese, and scrambled eggs, carefully forking them around the slippery and shiny meattube that oozes steamy drops of grease onto her plate.

Each day, we converse the best we can, trading laughs and makeshift stories as the morning fog dissipates and the sky brightens up. During the breakfast routine, when our gracious benefactor has her eyes elsewhere, Christine deftly wraps her blanched wiener in a napkin, pockets it (as to not offend by leaving it untouched), and tosses it aside later on. In truth, it's a bit of an awkward routine, but we have passed the point of trying to politely say *no thanks*. After going through this polite-but-questionable routine for a few days, Christine has something of a light bulb moment. In Listvyanka, as in many parts of Russia, there are countless packs of stray dogs roaming in and about the town. If anyone would appreciate a boiled tube of unknown meat, it would be them.

After warming up from our icy plunge, we head into the kitchen, wrinkling our noses at the aroma. The routine goes off without a hitch and Christine pockets her meat as per usual. We excuse ourselves from breakfast and step out into a dreary morning, with cold drizzle misting under the haze of an ashen sky. Walking up one of the many unmarked roads, Christine is visibly excited as she calls the dogs that trot up and down the alleys. One by one, they come sniffing about; they've caught wind of the mystery meat sitting in Christine's outstretched hand. The few stray dogs that have caught the sausagey-scent multiply within moments. At least a dozen dogs of bastard breeds are now surrounding her, waiting to see what offerings will be presented to their canine militia. The very instant Christine exposes her luke-warm wiener to the crowd, they swarm. She can't take a step without a dog impeding her, and the larger ones starting to jump and bark. Engulfed in an angry sea of flea-infested fur, Christine panics. She starts calling out for help but I am already bent over and crippled with laughter, unable to do much but shake my head at her oh-too-predictable predicament. As the hounds of Lake Baikal begin to leap and snap, I watch the situation disintegrate from comical to borderline dangerous. The begin to maul her, desperately clawing. I shout to her over the yapping horde.

"THROW THE MEAT AND RUN!"

I don't think that will be a sentence I ever yell again, and the ludicrousness of it isn't lost on me.

She hucks the meat down the lane, escaping into the opposite direction as the dogs spring into action. They hunt down every last morsel of hot meat scattered around the lane, barking and biting over the dirty scraps. Christine catches her breath at my side, red in the face, thanking her lucky stars she didn't lose a finger to the dire wolves of the Russian steppe.

As for me, I just keep laughing.

Chainsaw Bridges, Vodka Streams

Irkutsk. A part of me can't believe I'm here. I confess, I know absolutely nothing about the place, save one important tidbit: it's a territory on the board game RISK. It's a game I played quite often growing up, a staple of weekends with friends and family reunions. Now, I can't tell you the size of the city, nor whether or not it has any noteworthy historical significance. Is it a factory town? An entrepreneurial hub? Was it here where the Russian flag was first designed or where the Soviets crafted their national anthem? Of these, I have no clue. What I do know is that Asia (that's the green continent on the board, folks) is worth 7 troops per turn if you own the whole continent. And you can't own the continent without Irkutsk. Or Yakutsk. Or Kamchatka, for that matter. Growing up, these places with funny names never seemed real to me. They were almost removed from reality, disconnected by way of their foreignness. As far as the RISK board goes, I'm about as far from home as the map allows. Never in a million years would my twelve-year-old self have thought I'd be here.

Yet here I am.

As I wander the surprisingly-busy streets I can't help but wonder: if I had never played RISK would I have still chosen to stop here on my Trans-Siberian Adventure? Would I even have embarked on one? *Ir-kut-sk*. *Ear Cootsk*. Probably? I honestly don't know, but as I wait at what I hope is a local bus terminal I trace the lines of memory backward. When was it decided that I would come here? What threads of my life were woven together to get me from playing RISK at my wobbly, oft-stained kitchen table in Napanee, Ontario, Canada to *here?*

I'm lost in the causes and effects of my life. It's a mess of connections, comings and goings. We missed a train in Yekaterinburg a few days ago, and I can't help but ponder the consequences that will have for the rest of my life. The experiences and impressions, opportunities both had and missed. Multiply that by some odd trillion and you have that mess that we call life. As my ass starts to get sore from sitting on the hard cement outside the bus station, I'm realizing once more that it's all just a crap shoot.

And I don't even know how to play craps.

I shake away the webs of bewilderment and set my thinking to Ulan-Ude, our next destination. We're stopping there for two simple reasons: it is the hub of Buddhism in Russia and there is a giant head of Lenin in the city square. As a Buddhist, I should probably be looking forward to the eclectic and exotic temples, the varied histories of the practice on the steppe...but the giant head of Lenin is too peculiar to not think about. Fortunately, it's then that our bus arrives.

By "bus" I of course mean "crowded twelve-seat van with one working door that is more rust that automobile." The sliding door creaks open before us and we uneasily pile in, our giant backpacks crammed between our legs. The unfamiliar process highlights our foreignness here in Siberia, and we stand out against the silent Russians that sit motionless around us. I scavenge some coins from my pocket and pass the money forward, clueless to the amount we need to pay. I let the driver pick out the coins he needs from my outstretched palm as he waits to weave back into the congested traffic. We pass a few other handfuls of rubbles forward as well, the middlemen in a chain of debt as other passengers pile in behind us. No one asks, they just reach toward us with a handful of coins and we oblige. They offer no smiles, no thank yous. It's an obligatory act, one seemingly beyond the expectation of social niceties.

Sitting near the front of this oxygen-starved clown car, and hindered by our bags, we really have no idea who else is in the cramped shuttle with us, no clue whose hands are passing us money. Pressed against Christine, I can barely inch my head around to take in the scene. I do notice there is a woman to my immediate rear who looks vaguely professional, and I offer her a friendly smile. She offers none in return. As for the man beside me, he reeks of vodka. It' not even 10 a.m.

Oh, and he is wielding a chainsaw.

Instead of a backpack at his feet, this man has a fully-functional chainsaw resting between his legs.[23] The fresh scent of gasoline wafts throughout the van as we bump and bounce along a busy, pockmarked road. The icing on this cultural cake, however, is not his coordinated wardrobe — a stereotypical Adidas sweat suit and complimentary gold chain — but the overwhelming stench of booze emanating from his very being. I wrinkle my nose at the gas/vodka combination. Locked into the van — and without a seatbelt — there isn't much I can do but chuckle, shrugging off my budding concern with a *let's-see-where-this-goes* sense of curiosity. It's that sense of willingness that usually leads to a decent story. Or an early death.

As we roll along, stopping every now and then to allow folks to hop on or off, the chainsaw bounces lazily between the man's knees. I lean away, tilting my head every time it rolls my direction, the gnarly teeth inching ever closer to my jawline. The owner seems to be paying it no heed, preferring to distract the driver with some boisterous, one-sided conversation. He has a half-broken cigarette in his mouth, unlit and dangling, as he barks away in slurred Russia. That one-sided conversation, much like his distinct odours, eventually makes its way to me.

Between the accent, the slur, and the mutual lack of lingual parity I don't catch most of his incoherent question. I pull the standard smile and nod, conveying my support of his unknown questioning in hopes that he returns to talk-yelling at the driver. Which he does not.

I glance to my co-passengers, hoping someone can potentially translate the question that is once more lobbed in my direction. Everyone on the bus averts their eyes, leaving me to my fate. I stare at him blankly, putting my hand up to prevent the blade from knocking out some teeth. The chainsaw-wielding local doesn't seem to take no for an answer, goading a woman into translating for him. Her face and neck redden in blotchy patches as she stutters to speak up.

"He vants to know vhere you are from."

Her accent is thick but her English is almost perfect. I'm curious as to why she never spoke up before, but I don't have time to dwell. I reply, enunciating extra loud and extra slow…because that always works.

"I'M FROM CANADA."

He rambles off another incoherent volley and this time my translator doesn't feel like deciphering his response. He tries to coax her into facilitating our conversation, but to no avail. With a gesture, and possibly a heavily-accented word (though it could just be some odd drunken gargle) he makes clear his next topic of conversation: hockey. I cross my fingers that he isn't intending to rehash the Summit Series with the help of a poorly-oiled Russian chainsaw. I gesture that I comprehend, miming a slap shot. He gets disproportionately excited, shooting off a half paragraph of nonsense before my stupefied look reminds him of my linguistic ignorance. He mimes a slap shot in return, giving me a friendly body check that catches me by surprise. He's laughing now, face red and shoulders bouncing.

And then he stops, silent. I try not to stare, but we're awash in awkward. I think he's mentally pulled the goalie, so to speak.

Resting both hands on the dirty blade he sits motionless for just a moment too long, lingering wherever his mind has drifted off to. He is searching for a word, it turns out, and an important one at that. He squints, as if closing his eyes will fire his brain into overdrive. His eyebrows slide up, and then down, and then up again. It's equal parts comical and worrisome. *Is he having a heart attack?*

All of a sudden, he snaps back to our mini-bus reality, hands now stained with grimy smudges. He stares straight into my eyes, offering an honest smile. A connection. He holds the stare, intense and semi-glazed, but kind. With no hands on the chainsaw it bounces and falls against the seat in front of him. He doesn't notice, doesn't care. He extends a calloused hand, dirty and broad. Drawing out a single drunken word, he lets it fall heavy as he offers me a slow thumbs up. The word creeps out at Zamboni speed.

"Reespekt"

I return the universal gesture with a nod and an honest smile. And yes, respect.

bastard days and breadcrumbs,
blowtorch horrors on a weathervane pyre
paper thin and modest
a brand-new map to haunt us
a swansong killing field

Flotsam on the Hurricane Wall

A Lesson in Letting Go

She pukes. Not even thirty minutes into a bus ride easily outpaced by a snail, and she pukes. It fills a clear, thin bag and I see the chunks press against its sides. Bulges of white-pink float in a bile soup. I can almost feel them through the plastic. Immediately the smell wafts through the cramped vehicle, and I can't help but laugh. Christine, on the other hand, is fighting off the urge to chuck up her own breakfast in response to the pungent smell. We aren't even out of Beijing yet.

It is our second trip to the Chinese capital, and our first time heading to the Greatest of Walls. We found ourselves in the metropolis in 2012 in what was a dreary, snow-dusted November. Having set our sights on the wall of walls we were disappointed when we were told the buses weren't running because the snow had closed the tourist sections of the wall. How a few centimeters of snow could shut down 5,000km of wall I will never quite understand. The scheming scammers still attempted to lure us into an overpriced and ill-fated taxi ride but we shrugged off their insistences and headed back to our hostel, wall deprived.

Fast forward to 2014, and we are once again in the smoggy maelstrom of Peking. My lungs instantly regret our visit, the dirty, humid air sticking to my insides like tar. Unlike the desolate Beijing of winter, summer Beijing is a booming, bustling sprawl of humans packed liked sardines within the narrow and tumultuous *hutongs* of the old city. It is the Golden Week, and we are officially idiots.

The Golden Week in China is essentially the one week of the year where everybody and their dog takes a holiday. The sweltering powder-keg of a city, with its 21 million residents, has just ballooned to include the visiting masses from all around the People's Republic. There is, quite literally, no escape: we cannot book a train or plane or bus out of Beijing because they are all full. We ask the hostel to double and triple check our searches, hunting for any faint hope of freedom on the staccato Wi-Fi that chugs along at dial-up speeds. Our nearest exit is a flight to Chengdu, in 6 days. Six. Days. Almost a week of pushing and shoving and dodging through impermeable crowds when all we want is another little peak of the hectic city before exploring the calmer spaces of the country. Alas, no such luck is bestowed upon us. Lesson learned.

With nothing to be done, we make the best of it, exploring and shopping and haggling our way across the sprawl. The Great Wall is once again within our reach, leaving us to ponder our options: do we want to take the tourist approach, a calmer, quieter tour on a secluded piece of the wall? Or, do we want a cheaper bus ride to the less-secluded (read: chaotic beyond all reason) portion? We are already drowning in the free-for-all mob, sacrificial victims to the jackhammer pandemonium. We decide to say to hell with the scenic, quiet, private tour. We want to see the wall how the Chinese see the wall, to experience it in their shoes as much as possible. We pack our day bags and fumble our way to the bus stop, relying on vague memories of our previous visit to safely guide us to the terminal. We brace ourselves for the chaos.

In for a penny, in for a pound.

We arrive to unadulterated insanity. Bus after bus pulls into the parking lot, packs itself full of paying tourists, and goes about its way in a never-ending queue that stretches across the paved lot and onto the multi-lane road. We are no strangers to an overcrowded bus ride, of course, and so we stay the course. It should come as no surprise, however, that "crowded" in China has its own meaning. We nudge our way into the mass, elbows out. This is China, after all. Canadian niceties will get you nowhere.

Engulfed in the rabble, we are ever-so-slowly herded toward one of the buses. Christine and I are some of the last to be boarded and we have to hunt for seats...but there are none to be found. We discover, after being ignored and waved off by an attendant, that we must stand for the duration of the ride. There are a few dozen others — all Chinese — who are forced to stand as well. I furrow my brow, casually leaning on the nearest seat as I look around for some guidance. I try to point out to the bus-filler/ticket-taker that I paid for a seat but she ignores me, the bus starting to roll out of the lot. Fortunately, it's a short ride.

Or, it usually is. In the vicious traffic snarls of Golden Week, we spend an hour just making it a handful of kilometers, leaving our feet sore before we even arrive to hike along the wall.

The young couple sitting beside us are now leaning down, the young man comforting his partner with a classic back pat as she rests her head against the seat, puke bag at the ready. Off and on for the duration of our trip — which is stretching toward the two-hour mark — she chucks her cookies, bag brimming as her stomach empties. The bus is stifling, the odours questionable. The collective body heat of a hundred people only adds to the oppression of an autumn Beijing. Our feet begin to cramp as we switch positions. Squatting, leaning, two-handed leaning — anything to shift the discomfort. I'm breathing solely through my mouth, ignoring the bouncing sack of vomit to my immediate left. Christine is going pale from the bumpy bus ride and its upchuck aroma.

By now we are marinating in the pukey stench, basking in our own dripping sweat which trickles down our arms and legs.

We arrive much like we left: in a massive parking lot crawling with tourists. Our bodies are yearning for movement as we push our way off the bus and into the "fresh" air, shuffling toward the ticket line. It is, I confess, more of a mass than a line; a blob of people nudge their way to the forefront with no discernible organization or sense of respect. Disorganized anarchy is the only way to describe it, and my brain fails to compute the lack of reasoning. Lines would speed up the entire process, improve the flow of pedestrian traffic, and generally minimize the frantic rush to get a ticket. They would also, I suppose, detract from the whirlwind of chaos that envelopes the place. Maybe chaos is what they are going for.

We make it to the front of the "line" with a few friendly shoulder shoves and elbow jabs, securing our tickets (and probably a few bruises). We finally outpace the feral crowd, walking against the slope that leads us ever-closer to the wall. We work to dodge other visitors, though the real hazard is their lunches.

Fried mystery meats on wooden sticks poke out in every direction from the crowd, and the constant risk of being jabbed by *whatever-on-a-stick* leads me to walk with my hands constantly raised in anticipation of a wayward jab. Our feet crunch on the broken bits of wood littered by the tourists, the entire area cluttered with garbage as we progress through the disarrayed tourist trap. I watch countless visitors — all Chinese — toss their refuse straight onto the ground. Every garbage bin is heaping, and recycling containers are nowhere to be found. Empty bottles and soda cans line the base of the wall as we approach the monument. The faded green grass is rife with bits of wood and plastic dropped from tourists above, yet never collected. It rests in wind-blown piles, a sea of trash crashing against the wall. Simply put, the place is a disgusting mess.

We stride up the first sets of stairs, eyeing the wall as it rolls over the hills before our eyes, expanding into the distance as far as we can see. Every inch is dotted by specks of tourists, like ants upon a mound. The garbage, alas, doesn't end as we come out into the open. We notice it speckled all along the base of this great monument to human ingenuity and human suffering, a disappointing addition to the sheer epicness of this World Wonder. The crowd meanders up and along the wall, and we have to fight to find a spot less tourist-dense, trekking over the steeper inclines for a few square inches of our own. It's hard to tell from the photos, but the wall is damn steep. It bends and curves to its terrain, and we work up a sweat as we wander and explore. We trek past the worst of the crowds, though they are truly inescapable. Visiting the wall on China's terms leaves us in an unavoidable throng of people, all cherishing their few days of reprieve as they snap photo after photo, ignorant to the horde ever at hand.

Looking around, we are waist deep in an ocean of people, all churning and crashing. There is no escape, and by now none is needed. As the wind kicks up, the red flags along the wall snap and crack to life. One by one they ripple against the expansive backdrop, dancing in the disarray.

It's our cue: we give in.

We accept the absurdity of the terms that have been given, that we are but flotsam writhing in a sea of disorder; we are the calm within the storm around us, witnesses to an indescribable chaos. It claws at us, torrential and unrelenting, a tumultuous ocean. All we can do is let go.

It consumes whole.

~~~~~

They say you can see the Great Wall from space. That's actually false, but it doesn't matter. Because from space you don't feel the nudges of people shoving past as you wait in line. You don't feel the angle of the incline in your knees as you scale its length and width. From space, you don't have to dodge greasy sticks of meat nor the clueless tourists who wield them. You don't see the garbage blowing against the stone, caught gusts of in mini-tornadoes. You don't hear the ups and downs of a complex foreign language. For all of that and more you need to be *here*. *Now*.[24]

~~~~~

We get seats for the ride back to the city. No one pukes. In the madhouse hurricane of the Golden Week that is a simple blessing well received.

Next time, though, we're taking the damn tour.

The Dogs of Nam

A Lesson in Culture Shock

I heard this story from a friend of mine I met in Cambodia. She was a New Zealander whom I spent a few days exploring Siem Reap with before we each went our separate ways. During the inevitable talk about food in Asia we came to the grim topic every backpacker will find themselves both discussing and witnessing: the consumption of cats and dogs. While that shit wouldn't stand in North America and Western Europe (even though Western countries justify eating other animals) it certainly is common in Asia. While I think killing can and should be avoided I also try and not judge cultures that are both different and less affluent than my own. Who knows? Roll the dice a little differently and that could be me living on the streets of Hanoi, doing whatever I must to keep my family fed and secure. Anyway, I've taken some creative liberties to flush out the details of how I envision this story happening. Real talk: it isn't for the faint of heart.

A young woman was backpacking around Asia when she found herself in the ramshackle chaos of Hanoi. A beautifully-disorganized city, she ended up aimlessly strolling up and down the Old Quarter, peeking down narrow alleys and into bustling stalls while avoiding the swarming scooters that zipped every which way. Waves of steam and pungent smoke washed over her as she weaved along the makeshift sidewalks, darting passed food stalls as she casually declined tuk-tuk rides at every street corner. She could smell stale beer as she waited on the corner, the stench hovering over a plastic bag full of dented Tiger's and half-crushed 333's, the

151

pissy odour wafting in the humidity. The remnants leaked out onto the curb to splash against the worn foam of her plastic flip-flops, no doubt made in a morally-questionable factory right there in South East Asia.

After pacing the helter-skelter alleyways, the woman came to a run-down, hole-in-the-wall restaurant. Open to the street, there were a few local patrons peppering the sidewalk on tiny plastic stools. Hunched over their minuscule tables, they clogged the non-existent flow of push-and-shove pedestrian traffic. The restaurant itself was rather nondescript: crowded shelves and poor lighting in the back combined with a few plastic tables and chairs in the front. Rounding out the scene was rectangular stove top with various pots and pans, manned by a balding Vietnamese cook, leathery and taut. What the woman noticed next, however, stopped her in her tracks.

The restaurant sold dogs. For eating.

Much like lobster tanks in the West, one simply walked up to the counter and pointed at the dog they wanted. The chatty-yet-stern proprietor would then prepare it fresh for you. Standing there, overtaken by a culture shock so unexpected, the woman eyed the tiny rusted cage. There was but one dog remaining — a little puppy.

Now, this woman loved animals. Ok, perhaps not *all* animals but certainly dogs. And super certainly puppies (who doesn't love puppies?). The view before her eyes tugged at her heart strings with such savage force that she immediately approached the counter and tried to communicate with the vendor. Unfortunately, he spoke no English and she spoke no Vietnamese. Dedicated to freeing this soon-to-be-eaten pup, she did her best to gesture to the man in hopes of trying to convey her desire to purchase the last remaining baby dog. He caught on quickly, and they worked to barter out a reasonable price. They went back and force flashing hand gestures before switching to her mobile phone where she hammered out the final exchange via a translation app and a calculator. They agreed on a price and the woman happily paid the man a fistful of Dong, knowing she had just saved the life of a small, cute, and helpless animal. What she would do with this little puppy, she had no clue. She was in the middle of a backpacking trip and really couldn't take a puppy with her...but that wasn't the point. The point was to prevent this dog from being killed. And she succeeded. Her heart was swelling, so much, in fact, that she was fighting back tears. *Maybe the world wasn't so fucked up after all.*

The man wiped his brow, the heat from the stove a constant assault. He tucked away the handful of bills in his pocket before popping open the lid of the cage. His bony hands reached in, wrapping around the cute little puppy as it pressed against the wire walls. The act of barking still unfamiliar, all it could do was whimper as it was plucked from the ground. Placing his other hand on the puppy's torso, the cook then snapped its neck, tossed it in a bag, and handed the meal to the horrified woman.

Because to him it was a meal, not a pet, and he assumed she was just going to cook it at home. This was take out.

The woman stood there, broken. She wept.

~~~~~

I, too, saw my fair share or terrible things in South East Asia. Without even getting into the historical fallout of the war, there were enough heart-wrenching scenes scattered about the country to keep me perpetually on edge. Jolts of culture shock, more like knives than electricity, stabbed deep. They are palpable and memorable, the kind of things you can't unsee and wrestle to comprehend...

I saw a man torching a dead dog on the sidewalk. Or what counted for a sidewalk, anyway.

It was in Vietnam, and my heart hurt. We had walked around the city of Hanoi for a few hours, dragging our feet around the capital as we introduced ourselves to the country. We ambled around dozens of small streets and bustling markets, sampling the ceaseless turbulence. While the markets were a great place for cheap fruits and cheap bread, they were also a hub for the sale of animals. Chickens and hens were the most common, many stalls dotted by cages crammed with the birds. The hand-crafted cages rested on wooden blocks or were left piled the road, shit and piss dripping from the wires as the animals squabbled and fought for space. While their panting and clucking was lost to the din of haggling locals and speeding mopeds, their smell drifted to mingle with the stench of rotting fruit and vegetables. Every footstep was awash in a new smell, the bastard concoction of odours — occasionally delicious but more often than not, questionable — a constant cultural onslaught. It was these sights, and their accompanying smells, we found both enriching and overwhelming. The tidal chaos of it all was inescapable.

It was shortly thereafter, strolling back to the Old Quarter, when I caught sight of a man cooking up a dog with a hand-held torch. I couldn't help but tense. I felt my stomach, and my heart, drop. My steps faltered but I kept walking. I did a double take, hoping my eyes were playing tricks.

They weren't.

I looked again, and again, staring as my throat tightened. As an outsider, it wasn't my place to judge the cultural norms of the country — so I didn't — but I felt a sickening tightness as I continued walking, a visceral sadness that nagged my steps for several days.

I will never unsee that sight, and it marks one of the many horrible experiences I have been witness to during my travels. Now, I have spent eleven years of my life working on a farm. I am no stranger to the fact that animals die every day for our consumption. I've seen it. I've smelled it. I've washed the blood from my hands, quite literally. I can assure you, watching an animal be killed before your very eyes, seeing them skinned and cooked is something very different from buying a pack of meat at your local grocery store. There is a connection; it becomes personal.

When I travel, I yearn for connection. The openness, the newness of a place and its people is what I love to bask in. Yet it often comes with a price.

In China, that price was watching a dog roast on a spit outside my hostel in Nanning. Parked out on the street, the thick smoke blew right into my face every time I passed. I didn't have the heart to mention this to Christine, whose love of dogs overshadows her love of, well, everything and everyone. I was left to bury the sorrow, helpless to the fetid breeze as it clawed at my lungs each and every time I stepped out into the hazy city air.

In Thailand, that price was the sound of my taxi running over a stray cat as we were shuttled to a subway station in Bangkok, the crunch and crush of bone felt audibly under the weight of my $3 ride. The hurried driver sent a side-glance my way to see if I noticed the lifeless corpse left in our wake as we weaved through the night. I did. I stared at him in shock, speechless and furious. He paid me no mind and kept driving, though I couldn't help but wonder how he felt. *Did he think we wouldn't notice? Did he care? Did he think WE didn't care, and thus kept driving?* I never told Christine about that either.

In Cambodia, that price was seeing entire families sleeping outside on dirty slabs of torn cardboard, hoping for charity from a city without any to offer. Children played with broken toys, kicking around pieces of garbage as their parents sat lost in their own hopelessness. A handful of the older generation were missing limbs, victims of Cambodia's violent past.

As someone who diligently avoids killing mosquitos and stepping on ants, I take *life* quite seriously. I treat living things the way I want to be treated — and I don't want to be murdered. I don't want to be caged, or eaten, or left to rot on the street, ignored. I will never judge someone for killing out of necessity as that's often a fact of life for many people around the world. I'm fortunate that I can live my life with minimal harm to those around me, animals included. I give thanks for that every day.

I'm not sure what the point of all this is. Maybe it's to serve as a reminder that travel isn't all #stokedwanderlust and sandal tans. It isn't all fun in the sun and wicked pics for your Instagram. Coming from North America or Western Europe, travel can be one hell of a wake-up call to the less-than-ideal conditions the overwhelming majority of the world is living in while you hostel-hop and barter for those shitty elephant pants.

More importantly, perhaps, it's a reminder that we could all likely step up our compassion. It's 2018. Do we still really need to be roasting animals on a spit...or, God forbid, with a blowtorch?

we'll chase the night,
an unkempt running through.
seized by chaos, we've clutched the dark
and the stray lights of a war-torn city
that hasn't slept in years

Miscellaneous Carpet Stains

A Lesson in Rolling with the Punches

Beijing. Again. Why do things never go right when I'm there?

After a week of seeing the sights, inhaling the noxious city air, and having everyone and their dog try to rip us off, Christine and I were heading to Chengdu for what we hoped would be a less busy, less crowded urban scene. I know, that's asking for a lot in China, but we had our fingers crossed and our thumbs held that some reprieve would find us.[25] After a few days of eyeing trains and planes and long-distance rickshaws, we secured a questionably-early flight out of Peking. It was so early, in fact, that it made sense for us to sleep at the airport. I figured we could grab a few hours of shut eye on a bench somewhere, briefly waking up to groggily amble through security before catching some z's on the plane. Hardly luxurious, but it would save us both money and time — and I'm a diehard fan of frugality. Christine, however, has standards. We (read: she) decided that we would "splurge" and get a cheap hotel for the night, one in close proximity to the airport with a shuttle and a real bed. Fancy, I know.

I jotted down the phone number for a hotel that met Christine's rigorous criteria while still being cheap enough to meet mine. We simply had to call them from the airport and they would come and get us. Easy peasy *níngméng* squeezy.

Except nothing is that simple in China.

We arrived at the airport and made our way to the information desk. We didn't have phones with us, and so we asked the young attendant to call the hotel on our behalf and request their shuttle. It was here that our plan began to derail.

The woman informed us in broken-but-comprehendible English that the phone number wasn't working. I politely asked her to try again, working that Oldfield charm as I leaned into the desk with a smile. She did, but no one answered yet again. She called once more. Same results.

Shit.

I tried to convey to Christine that this was, perhaps, a sign that we should simply stay here at the airport, curl up on the floor, and sleep away the inconvenience. It was then that the woman informed us — all too conveniently, I might add — that there was an equally cheap hotel nearby that she could arrange for us, with a shuttle to boot. After some skeptical questioning, it turned out that it wasn't quite as cheap, but it nevertheless seemed reasonable and so we agreed. In hindsight, the airport floor would have been infinitely preferable.

The woman called up the "hotel" and hastily chatted with someone. Our shuttle bus was on its way.

What arrived to pick us up could hardly be called a bus, however. It more closely resembled a van, but even that was a bit of a stretch.

Imagine, if you will, that a disorganized and unkempt serial killer used a minivan to collect his victims. Then, imagine if he hid that van in a junkyard for the better part of a decade. Continuing, imagine if someone found that van, wiped the dust off the windshield (but only windshield) and started using it as a commercial vehicle to transport human beings. You now have a vague idea of what our shuttle looked (and smelled) like. Luxury, indeed.

Fortunately, we were assured our "hotel" was close to the airport. We discovered, however, that "close" in China was a relative term — especially when it came to scamming tourists. Fifteen minutes later we were still driving, bouncing along some pot-holed back road with the hustle and bustle of Beijing disappearing into the cracked rear-view mirror. The glow of the city continued to fade, lost in the heavy shadows of our lightless street. Our driver, and his accomplice, remained silent. No small talk, no radio. Just the choking struggle of the run-down engine as it jostled the makeshift road, carrying us into the foreign night.

It was about this time that I unclipped my pocket knife.

A few minutes later we weaved around an empty parking lot and arrived at our destination. If I had to sum it up in a word, I think *sketchy as fuck* would be the most applicable. It was reminiscent of an old Soviet bunker, with crumbling rectangular pillars bearing the weight of its chipped and dated concrete facade. Curled up near the door was a mangy runt of a dog, a weary beast that looked just as haggard as the building's exterior. The interior fared no better.

Dank and dim, the lobby was far from the inviting space one conjures when thinking of a hotel. Here there were worn and stained carpets, dusty and cluttered desks, and a sizeable fish tank that had likely not been cleaned since the Cultural Revolution. Pressing my face against it like a curious child, I was unable to see what lurked within the swampy prison...assuming anything could even survive its algae-ridden depths.

The check-in process itself was brief but smooth, though that did little to reassure us of our circumstances. It also didn't boost our confidence that the police were present, interrogating a Tibetan monk in the first-floor hallway that overlooked the lobby. Everyone (read: the lone staff member at the desk) seemed to shy away from watching the spectacle as the officers verbally prodded the man, eventually following him into the confines of his budget accommodation. We didn't stick around to see what happened next.

Our room was on the second floor, down an empty, dark, and begrimed hallway. The corridor was lined by dented walls and ripped wallpaper, with a carpet that perhaps once shone bright red but now stood closer to the inviting colour of bloody stool. Years of dirt and dust and unknown stains had collected atop its wrinkled and frayed surface like scum on water. It would take a braver man than I to walk here in bare feet, and I gave thanks I wasn't wearing my sandals.

Our room — to our mutual surprise — was not cramped, though it was still a far cry from anything within the realm of luxury. It may have been borderline spacious but it certainly was not clean. Here, too, the wallpaper was peeling and marked by a lifetime of stains whose origins I'd rather not consider. Among the blotches and blemishes were the corpses of many a dead mosquito, smeared along the walls in tiny black and bloody splotches. They were a nice addition to the cob webs in the corners and the spider webs under the desk. I made it my job to keep as much of our possessions off the floor in hopes of minimizing contact with that toxic turf, placing our meagre possessions on the wooden chair and table. Our eyes then reluctantly turned to the bed. Our bags would be safe from whatever critters creeped and crawled in the night. The question was, would we?

The blankets on our double bed were old and well used but clean enough to not require an immediate burning. They were musty, but felt tolerable to the touch. We shook them out and no dead bugs (or worse) were revealed, which we considered a small but important victory. What was a much larger and infinitely more important victory, though, was the fact that we had a Western toilet. Sure, squatting makes the act of...uh, number 2ing easier but it is desperately hard on my knees for more than a few moments. And in all honesty, I would rather just sit down and relax when I'm taking a dump. Call me old fashioned.

In tandem with our magical Western toilet (one-ply toilet paper included!) was an electrical outlet AND a lamp. With that, our immediate and basic needs were covered. Admittedly, the shower was actually cleaner than some I used back in university and so I didn't bat an eye there.[26] I did, however, wear my sandals as I bathed because it sure as heck was not spotless. Mr. Clean — or whoever the Chinese equivalent was — would have a field day here. Or a heart attack.

Settled, though still uncomfortable with the whole situation, we threw open the heavy curtains to get a better sense of just where the fuck we were. The scene before us was, and I don't use this word lightly, shocking. Sure, in the distance was the rest of the sleepless capital city in all its light-polluting glory, but within the immediate vicinity of our hotel was a scene that could have easily — easily! — passed for the remnants of a war zone. The building behind us could not with any accuracy be called a building. It was a *ruin*. Cement and stone and wood all mingled with one another in a collapsed heap, garbage and scrap metal entwined every which way. There were even goats climbing around the wreckage, chewing on whatever bits of greenery poked through the mess. Had this been broadcast on CNN and touted as something from a warn-torn nation not a soul would bat an eye at the claim.

I was stunned. Suffice it to say, we kept the curtains closed for the rest of our stay.

Having now acclimatized to our suspect accommodation, we rustled through our packs to scavenge whatever bits of food and snacks we had collected...with disappointing results. At this hour, but more importantly in this area, we didn't really feel like wandering around in search of a restaurant or 7/11. It should go without saying that this place did not offer room service. With not even a vending machine to supply us with a sugary bite, we walked through the empty hotel to the front desk where we had seen some snacks and refreshments available for purchase. Unfortunately, and once again not surprisingly, there was nothing "fresh" about these refreshments.

Locked away in a smudge-ridden glass case in the lobby were a variety of snacks for sale. Most were Chinese in origin, and I couldn't even wager a guess as to what precisely they were. What caught my eye were the more recognizable items: off-brand Oreos and plain potato chips. It was a culinary jackpot. While hardly a delectable and nutritious meal, it would at least be a cozy and comforting snack to help us bide our time in the squalid flophouse. Having settled on our two-course meal, we waved over the solitary staff member to open the grubby case for us.

She refused.

She dismissed us with a few rapid sentences in Mandarin and continued about her duties, her attitude flippant enough to bridge the linguistic gap. The specifics were lost on us, and we were left to assume she didn't have the key for the case, or, that the cash register was closed for the night. The overarching tone, however, was that she was not going to open up the case for us. Period. So much for our romantic hotel dinner. Granted, it was probably for the best seeing as we could not read the best before dates, and the majority of the items were collecting dust...and Lord knows what else.

It was about then that we really began to realize the true nature of our predicament: we had been conned. Tricked into booking a night in a cesspool, we figured it would not be long until we were to be robbed and murdered and fed to the goats out back. Our tale would be used to chide fellow wanderers and anyone thinking of quitting their job to travel.

"Didn't you hear about that couple who was tricked," they'd say. "They went with strangers to a hotel where they were MURDERED TO DEATH!"

Alright, not exactly. But it was clear we were conned, that we had no food, and that we didn't feel safe. And so, as we settled into bed for the night to watch a movie and pick at the crumbs of our paltry snacks I made sure to lock the bolt on the door. I also made sure to jam our chair under the door handle. I kept my folding knife open and on the night table, just in case something went bump in the night. In hindsight, maybe it was a bit much, but at the time we really did not feel comfortable. My gut had been saying as much since the moment the hotel was booked, but I had brushed it aside.

We awoke the next morning to no actual problems. We were not robbed, we were not murdered, and we didn't get eaten alive by bedbugs or rodents. Pleasantly surprised, we packed up our things and had a safe but awkward and uncomfortable ride back to the airport in the "shuttle." We caught our flight and made it out of Beijing in one piece. Most importantly, we learned a few lessons.

First, always listen to your gut.

Second, speak up when you feel uncomfortable.

Third, always have accurate contact information for your accommodation.

Fourth, for the love of God, never, ever travel without snacks.

Breaking the Iceland

A Lesson in Silver Linings

"Well you know, for me personally, I just don't really like the Muslim people. I think, you know, they are barbarians..."

I would have face palmed, but I was driving.

Here we go...

She continued her rant a bit longer, seemingly oblivious to her blatant racism and heavy-handed discrimination. I kept my eyes on the road as we weaved out of Reykjavik toward the Golden Circle, wincing at her choice of an opening topic of conversation. We were four strangers in a tiny rental car about to embark on a ten-day trip around Iceland together.

So much for breaking the ice.

The rest of us let her finish her piece, for the most part, politely chiming in with our collective rebuttals as often as we could. Our group had assembled online before the trip, an impromptu collection of travellers from around the world all looking to explore the Land of Elves. Representing Europe was my co-pilot, a stout and outdoorsy Austrian who did push-ups for fun (and I mean that literally: he would do push-ups for fun whenever we stopped the car). Having grown up a stone-throw away from where Arnold Schwarzenegger was born, this was not all that surprising. He was intelligent and soft spoken, sharing my love of music and film and writing. We hit it off immediately.

Joining him from the Old World was a tough-as-nails gal from France, whose knack for taking incredible photos I envied. She was sporty and energetic, always up for adventure. Rounding out our travel quartet was our Chatty Cathy American, the woman who brought together this whole travel fellowship. After her opening salvo of awkward (read: racist) conversation it was clear that my North American comrade — in the grand tradition of travel stereotypes — was out of place. Her ridged views (and several over-packed suitcases) were already making the car feel cramped. In her meagre defence, it was a Toyota Yaris so there wasn't much room to begin with.

In hindsight, it's almost hilarious how different she was from us. Almost. In those bountiful spaces where it wasn't comical, however, it was downright puzzling and uncomfortable. She was the cultural antithesis to our group, and to the very notion of being a respectful traveller. Where we were calm and open and relaxed, she was a whirlwind of impatience and passive aggressiveness. Where we all kept our agreed-upon itinerary in mind, she worked ceaselessly to make ill-considered changes on short notice. Obsessed with Facebook and vee-logging (she refused to say vlogging), our Miss Adventuress was hyper connected to her phone. It was glued to her fingertips at all hours of the day, the rapid clicking of her texts ever-present in the background. As the three of us hunted for waterfalls and pined for adventure, she was perma-concerned with her battery life and the quality of her selfies. Not surprisingly, her digital obsession led to a stark disconnect from our actual travels — and from the group itself. Like many travellers these days, her investment lay not in exploring or making connections, but in documenting a seemingly superficial version of her trip. It was clear after the first day that the three of us didn't jive with her social media pseudo-travel. We all knew it — including her.

Which was peculiar, since it was she who brought us

disparate travellers together. We had all exchanged messages, and even Skyped before the meet-up…yet here we were, neck deep in a cultural bog that tasted a lot like quicksand.

As our trip progressed around the island I found myself genuinely curious as to how she had managed to get this far in life and, well, still be alive. I was bewildered by her social ignorance, struggling to rein in my own judgemental attitude. This was not (and I found this quite surprising) her first trip abroad. Yet within the inaugural fifteen minutes of our journey she had already absentmindedly led us off course — twice! How had she managed prior? In a rare moment of psychological weakness, I turned to my down-to-earth Austrian companion to ask that very question out of sheer disbelief that such a cluster fuck of a traveller could exist. It was like discovering a new species, one poorly designed to leave home yet who nevertheless ventures out the door, ignorance in tow, banking more on luck than any sort of research or preparation. I was both shocked and perplexed.

As travellers, we often wander to see, to experience, to engage, to feel. We want to set foot in foreign lands so we can breathe the air, witness cultures other than our own, and learn about ourselves and the world we live in. We travel to connect the dots. Anything less, I would argue, is doing a disservice to ourselves and those very places we visit.

By not connecting those dots, our American Miss Adventuress had absolutely no sense of reality, of what was socially acceptable. As a Canadian, I'm perhaps hypersensitive to my social environment, perpetually mindful of the needs of those around me, ever afraid of causing offence. I believe that as we travel, especially in groups, it's important to balance the needs of everyone involved. Without that concern for those around you, travel becomes an overly-selfish act, an exercise in getting exactly what you want.

As we drove the ring road, I tried to understand the mental

framework from which our American was experiencing the trip. I didn't want to judge her behaviour harshly, as difficult as that was, without first making an attempt to deconstruct and understand her perceptions. But what do you do when someone is incessantly clueless and persistently ignorant? When someone's negative behaviour affects the well-being of those around them?

After a few days, it came to a head.

We had spent the better part of an hour crawling up a rocky road toward Dettifoss, reputed to be the most powerful waterfall in all of Europe. I'm not precisely sure how a waterfall earns that title, but it sounded impressive and I was told not to miss it. The road was allegedly rated for cars (as opposed to being an F-Road, for off-road vehicles) so we made the drive, swerving around jagged rocks and cavernous potholes at little more than a snail's pace. Every few feet brought a new opportunity for a flat tire, my eyes darting back and forth to make sure we avoided disaster. It was a tedious drive, but the prize that awaited us was well worth the trouble.

With us was a hitchhiker we had picked up earlier in the day, a jovial ginger from Down Under who was spending a few weeks camping around the island. He was a pleasant addition to the crew, albeit just for the day, and we traded stories about his adventures. Emanating from him was not the most pleasant of aromas, as living in the brush takes something of a toll — understandably so. Our American Miss Adventuress complained about it the whole way, her jabs going from subtle to blunt faster than a New York minute. So blunt were her comments, in fact, that the Aussie regularly offered to leave because he felt bad and was embarrassed. The rest of us shrugged it off, par for the course of adventure, insisting that he stay. After a few weeks hiking and camping in the Icelandic bush, I doubt anyone would smell like Herbal Essences.

Miraculously, we didn't burst a tire on our way to Dettifoss, and we arrived at an indescribable view. The raging current rolled and rumbled in the background as we edged closer. No barriers blocked the disastrous cliff edges so we inched our way as close as our stomachs could handle. Splashes of icy spray dotted our faces and jackets as we hunted for elusive rainbows in the canyon, watching them come and go, dancing colours in the shifting light. It was majestic and powerful, primal and untamed. The way it should be.

After soaking up the view I roamed the area looking for better angles to take some photos. I caught up with our Miss Adventuress just as she gingerly stepped over one of the few barriers, ignoring the handful of warning signs. She was hunting for the perfect selfie.

As she switched from one embarrassing pose to another, she trampled the fragile grass beneath her shifting feet while simultaneously ruining the photos of a dozen other visitors whose view she now blocked. I politely pointed out her no doubt accidental carelessness but was sharply brushed off, a non-digital nuisance to her self-indulgent ego fest.

I confess, I was tempted to just shove her off the edge and be done with it.

The final straw came a couple days later. Having arrived at a cozy hostel along the windy coast of the Snaefellsnes peninsula, we checked into our accommodation with just enough time to catch some live local music. As we saddled up to the bar to watch the performance, our wayward companion intrusively wandered about the room "vee-logging." Her voice carried loud enough to rival the microphoned singer, her camera forced in the faces of both the audience and performers. She was a one-woman show, a tornado wearing H&M.

It is precisely this careless attitude I am not keen to tolerate.

As travellers, we are responsible for respecting the places we visit, and the people that inhabit them. This is non-negotiable in my book. I have seen too many jerks in too many countries flagrantly disregard local customs and socially-accepted behaviours that I have drawn the line. The cluelessly careless need to be reined in, need to be reminded that the world doesn't revolve around their hashtag vanity. If you are going to go somewhere but not actually *be there* then you might as well save yourself the time and stay home.

After her intrusive live and in concert vee-log, we dragged her to the back of the room and politely, but in no uncertain terms, told her that such behaviour really wasn't acceptable. Later that night she made plans with a different set of travellers. The next morning, she was gone.

I wish I could say that was the end of it, but her and I had booked an Airbnb together for our final night in Iceland. I can't say it was a comfortable stay, but she was decidedly less chatty...

Now, I'm perhaps being a bit harsh here but what I'm getting is this: sometimes people suck. Of course, not everyone is meant to be BFFs with everyone else. We all have our preferences when it comes to who we want to spend our time with and that's perfectly okay. We generally weed those individuals whom we don't particularly like out of our lives — or at the very least we try to. While it's important to always look for the best in people, sometimes there are individuals you will meet who are simply toxic to your health. Unfortunately for you, these people travel and you will, at one point or another, run into them. Maybe you will be lucky and just be stuck beside someone for a few hours, perhaps on an awkward flight or an uncomfortable train ride. If you're unlucky, you'll be stuck with them for longer, say for ten days in a tiny clown car as you road trip around a small island. But you roll with the punches. You develop patience. You learn to see the silver lining.

Because without her, our group wouldn't have come together. She was the driving force behind our unification, cobbling us from online strangers into an Icelandic fellowship. Because of her, I shared an incredible adventure with people who are now friends of mine for life. She prodded us into booking our accommodation early and got us hammering out an itinerary which took us to some of the most surreal and mystifying landscapes in the entire world. She may have been self-centered and out of touch with, well, everything, but without her our road trip adventure would have went smoothly.

And where is the fun in that?[27]

Christopher Kevin Oldfield

the hills sung welcome home
an unforgiving melody
lashed to the histories of a thousand lands
etched unencumbered
onto the atlas of this fire-fed soul

Christopher Kevin Oldfield

Watertown Sad: The Life and Times of Ricky Swordfire

A Lesson in…Honesty?

The first time I deliberately broke the law was when I was a kid. Sure, I broke the rules — or, rather, cleverly bent and twisted them to suit my devilish needs — but "the law" was a higher authority. If caught, I wouldn't just get grilled by my parents, I would get locked away in juvy until I was old enough to be sent to federal prison. Once there, I would waste away until the End of Days. Conveniently, my hometown had a jail right in town. It was aptly placed as a reminder to any small-town, would-be delinquents. Thankfully, I never set foot within its walls.

While my childhood is a foggy, nostalgic blur, I'm sure I couldn't have been more than 12 when I first tested Fate and broke the law. I happened in my local convenience store, a corner store that I visited almost daily. It was the place my pocket change went to die, coughed up in fair exchange for the coveted penny and nickel candies of the 1990's. It was heaven, sugary and sweet.

One day, as my brain tallied up the congealed tidbits in my mini paper bag, factoring in the proper tax to make sure I could afford my addiction, I deftly reached into one of the plastic bins and stole a candy. It was a five-cent piece: a blue shark. I was now, officially, a criminal.

At this point in time the store was owned by my aunt and uncle so I really could have just asked for a free candy if I was so desperate. They would have happily obliged — I was just a kid, after all. But I didn't. I just took the shark on a whim and ate it when I was out in the parking lot. #yolo

While that may have been the first time I broke the sacred social contract it certainly was not the last.

~~~~~

Under the watchful gaze of a hundred security cameras and fully-armed guards, I eased my foot off the brake, rolling my borrowed car forward to the painted yellow line. STOP was painted in attention-grabbing letters on the road, as if the tense atmosphere (and numerous other signs) didn't make things clear. I waited at the line, rehearsing my speech. For the first time in a long time, my university degree was proving itself useful. I studied theatre, and was about to give the performance of a lifetime. As the car ahead of me began to creep onward I was waved forward. It was my time to shine.

I was at the border between The Great White North and the US of A, the traffic at a congested standstill. Bomb-sniffing dogs padded up the lanes as border agents peered under cars with extended mirrors. If there is an opposite to "fun" and "carefree" it's the border to America. It is a laugh-free zone, an awkward and oozing field of anxiety. On my previous visit to the US, the border guard grilled me about my job — being a farmer — as if my "radical" choice of employment somehow threatened the very existence of his nation. I didn't bother to cross my fingers for a more receptive guard this time around, as I doubted any existed. Here at the border to the US, it's their job to prod, to intimidate. Few borders in the world are guarded more securely, though whether that results in a "safer country" is debatable. I've been to many of the safest countries in the world, and none had borders protected so aggressively. With such extensive security, you'd expect America to be a safe haven, free from the myriad crimes that plague most countries. Yet it isn't even in the top 100 safest countries. And here I was knocking at its gates.

Dozens of cars were backed up behind us, all eagerly awaiting a chance to enter Uncle Sam's backyard. More specifically, we were about to enter the cosmopolitan playground of upstate New York. A mere hundred metres ahead was the start of the American Dream and the endless and absurd possibilities that it offered up. Bargain box stores, low-cost gasoline, all-you-can-shoot firearms, Olive Gardens. America had it all.

Unfortunately, we weren't heading across the border to shop (though I intended to snag a few bags of groceries and fill up on gas while I was there). We weren't going to party, nor were we heading out into the wide world on some sort of YOLO road trip. We were simply going to pick up some mail.

This entire undertaking was the brainchild of my friend — it was his mail, after all — whose real name I won't use since he broke the law with crafty premeditation. When I mentioned I was going to write about our daring escapade, I asked if he wanted me to use a fake name for this story and, if so, what he would want that name to be. He replied with an unsettling lack of hesitation.

"Rick Swordfire, a bisexual Pisces who likes analingus."

"..."

"If the rest can't make it, go with Ricky."

"Ricky it is."

Now, my dear friend Ricky had ordered a rather expensive item which, if shipped into Canada, would costs thousands of dollars in import taxes. Naturally, he was okay with paying his fair share taxes — that's the price of living in a society, after all. But having to pay a bucket full of money just to move a personal item or two over an invisible border? That seemed an egregious affront to his politics and his pocketbook. Having spent every last cent on these purchases, Ricky S. wasn't keen to scrape up the financial dregs of his savings, pocket lint and all, and mail it off to The Man. Crafty son of a bitch that he is (he's a Pisces, after all) he devised a Plan B.[28]

With a few friends in tow, we would take a rental car to 'Murica, have a grand ol' time shopping, returning to Canada after a few days "holiday" — with his mail, of course. No suspicions would be raised, no heavy-handed tax dollars paid. Everyone would be happy...except the government, I guess, since we were technically robbing them. But whatever.

The first hurdle we encountered was that the two friends we invited to allay the suspicions of the border agents cancelled. In order to offset the questionable nature of two young men driving into the US alone we had hoped to drag some female friends with us. They bailed at the last minute, leaving us to commence the operation alone.

The second hiccup we encountered was at the border. As we crossed into the US, the border agents decided to search our car. Thoroughly.

We were asked to pull over to the side by a gruff and grim-looking border agent. It was there where the border guards combed over every inch of our vehicle. Dogs gorged on our questionable odours while mirrors illuminated every hidden nook of the undercarriage. The hood was popped and the engine scrutinized. The trunk, too, was investigated. Each of our packs were opened, scanned, and shoved back together. All while we stood nearby waiting room. With locked gates. And armed guards. Lots of them.

Welcome to America.

Nothing, of course, was found during their search, though oddly enough they never searched *us*. As the agents wasted American tax dollars in their hunt for contraband, Ricky and I simply chilled out in the guest corral, an area under constant watch by both staff and video surveillance. The majority of the remaining agents were across the room, chatting it up as if we didn't exist. Decked out with hand guns and machine guns and bullet-proof vests, they enjoyed a casual morning coffee as we sat uncomfortably on cold metal chairs, basking in the irony of the situation.

After playing host to us for a lagging thirty minutes, we were discharged, free to roam the highways and byways of the Land of Opportunity. Our eyes were set on Watertown, The Garland City, Jewel of the Empire State, and neither snow nor rain nor gloom of night would stay us.

Welcoming us along the open road were a growing host of billboards. As American as apple pie, they lined the interstate like toxic trees, spouting their noxious nonsense as we sped by. The prophetic scrawls served as a harbinger of box store deals, questionable legal advice, and the price of sin should we abstain from seeking forgiveness in the Lord. In short, everything a visitor to the US needs to know.

Under a lingering grey sky, we arrived at our foreign locale. The city itself wasn't too different from small-city Canada, the atmosphere a depressing and subtle mix of downtrodden and blasé. It was bland, satisfactorily generic. Fast food chains dotted each intersection, box stores and shopping centres having multiplied along the asphalt swaths in between. This was a cultural hotspot, a mecca of modernity luring folks in from the surrounding rural communities, as well as cash-savvy tourists from across the border. Unlike in Canada, here you could by booze in a convenience store and machine guns at the mall. It was unpretentious, unrefined, an-

Wait, machine guns at a shopping mall? That's fucked up.

I try not to judge people or places under the (probably correct) assumption that I'm not always right. But guns on display in a mall? That crosses something of a line, don't you think? Hunting rifles, arguably, are one thing, but having hand guns and automatic weapons normalized to such a degree that you can browse for them after hitting up a book store or buying some jeans at The Gap? Come on, America. You can do better. Also, since I'm already chiding you: use the Metric system. Like seriously. It's only you, Liberia, and Myanmar who use the Imperial system. Miles? Get your shit together.

Anyway.

Watertown offered us an unrefined urban landscape peopled by folks who I couldn't help but notice looked rather drab. Maybe it was just the day, or the weather. Maybe a local sporting team had just lost the big game. Whatever it was, there was palatable dullness to the place. It was in the air, a season you could breathe in. Uncomfortable, but manageable. It reminded me of wearing damp laundry; tolerable, but less than ideal. I thought it was just me, my own dumb filter altering my perspective. But Ricky agreed, and so we dubbed the unique dullness with an appropriate moniker: *Watertown sad*. It's that kind of existential *meh* that seeps into your soul, a chest-heavy exhalation equal parts desperation and indifference. It's that general sense of forlorn and predetermined disappointment, like drinking flat soda or eating a handful of chips thinking they are salt and vinegar but they turn out to just be plain. It's fine, but it's not what you had hoped.

Few things in that city were as *Watertown sad*, however, as our motel.

The Musty Inn, or whatever words were rusting out on the weather-worn sign, sat inelegantly in the foreground of a half-vacant strip mall. Queuing to check in were a clutch of soldiers, camo and all, no doubt on leave from the nearby army base. Their accents were as varied as the stains on the welcome mat, an interesting mix from every corner of the nation. Yes ma'am. No ma'am. Thank you, ma'am. American soldiers rival Canadians for extraneous manners. I felt right at home.

Having spent his final dime on the mail — and perhaps known for being on the frugal end of the spectrum — Ricky had booked us a cozy single room. With a single bed. Complimentary items included a rotary phone, cobwebs, a dubious aroma, and breakfast. We were now sitting pretty in the lap of luxury. I just hopped it wasn't contagious.

Picking up the mail was uneventful. It was mail, after all. We weren't running guns or smuggling drugs in clandestine orifices...this was just a glorified run to UPS.

Our reward for a job well done was an uncomfortable sleep in a tiny bed, wrapped in itchy wool blankets, the kind you'd find in flea-invested dog houses around the country. For a free breakfast, however, we tolerated the budget road house and all of its...charm?

The following morning, as we shoved our faces full of bleached carbs and "fruit drink" we plotted our re-entry into Canada, wary of our chances of making it home. We had been flagged already, and such a quick return would no doubt prompt suspicions. Would the rigorous security spot the items, or would they assume they had been there the whole time? Did they make note of everything we entered the country with during their search, or were they purely on the lookout for contraband?

As we mulled over our options, an outdated TV chattered on about the morning's news. Celeb highlights took the forefront, as per usual, spouting gossip as if it were revelations of national importance. A report on bed bugs came next, warning travellers to avoid cheap accommodations for fear of spreading the indestructible critters further abroad. The lone staff member restocking the no-name cornflakes failed to see the irony in the situation, leaving the TV on as the report droned on about the bug crisis. I made a mental note to check myself for bites after. I was already feeling itchy.

We took a final tour of the everyday city. Though it was awash in the promise of a new day, the urban expanse — and all contained within its concrete grasp — remained muted. Maybe it was hiding its vibrant secrets, its enriching marrow saved only for those willing to call the city home. Perhaps behind the veil of washed-out grey was unabashed majesty, a whirlwind of life. Maybe if I looked deep enough, I would see it.

Or perhaps the place was just meh. Watertown sad. But if the inhabitants were happy, I wasn't going to waste my energy worrying — I had another fish to fry.

As we worked our way north toward the border of Canada we played out various scenarios.

"Okay. So, if they ask about the…item, I'll just play dumb. I'm merely the hired wheelman on a weekend excursion."

"Wheelman? You're driving a four-door Hyundai. We might as well be taking the kids soccer practice."

While we had bought enough stuff to allay cursory suspicions, if the border agents had kept notes on our vehicle after their fact-finding mission we would likely be busted. What "busted" would entail was unknown. I could certainly downplay my involvement in Ricky's smuggling op, but I wasn't sure that would fly.

"Can you get vegan food in prison?" I wondered aloud.

"Maybe we can start a Meatless Monday."

It was then that I realized this whole adventure was a hilariously poor choice.

Back in line at the border, we once again inched our way toward the razor's edge. There were less cars, no patrolling dogs or visible guards toting sub-machine guns. Handing over our passports, Ricky waited in silence as I answered the polite agent's questions.

"What were you doing in the US?"

"Just a bit of shopping, picking up a few things."

My response was technically true — we did pick up a few things. It just so happened that we were transporting some of them illegally. But he didn't ask about that so I kept my mouth shut. Ricky leaned over to the window, adjusting his glasses as he waded in with his two cents.

"I bought some headphones at Best Buy."

Mental face-palm.

Time never stood still. My hands weren't clammy, my mind wasn't racing. Because it was already done. The agent handed back our passports, wishing us a good day. Now safe within the confines of the Great White North we made sure to play it cool until we were beyond their potential surveillance zone.

And then we laughed up a storm, impressed by the offhand success of our morally-questionable victory. We considered it a win for the little guy, for the Robin Hoods of the world. We had stormed the gates of Nottingham and managed to sneak away with a chest of untaxed riches, once again safe in Sherwood Forest.

Such were the life and times of Ricky Swordfire.

Christopher Kevin Oldfield

Bears Upon the Mountain

A Lesson in Being Prepared

I was nauseous by the time we got to the camp. The winding bus ride from Fujiyoshida to the Fifth Station of Mount Fuji was enough to leave me wide-eyed and wincing. It was the last bus of the day, and the beginning of our last-minute adventure to the summit of Fuji-san. I was in the midst of my third visit to the islands of Japan and I was determined to kiss the sky from the peak of that holy apex. My partner Christine and I had done zero preparation, of course, and we had only found out the day prior that we were about to climb it the "wrong way."

Back at the hostel, as we prepped our packs for the climb, we bumped into the cleaner of our little hostel. It was sweltering and sunny out, so she flashed us peculiar looks when he saw me wearing my headlamp.

"You are not going to climb Fuji-san now, are you?"

"Uhh….I mean, yes? Hai."

"No no no no no. You should climb tonight. It is the tradition."

And with that, she returned to sweeping, leaving us in a confused scramble to figure out what she meant. Tonight? Like, in the dark? For a country that prides itself on being sensible, that seemed like a pretty terrible idea.

Turns out, the cleaning lady was right.

A quick search online verified her claim. Traditionally, hikers leave during the evening and make the trek in darkness, arriving at the summit to witness the dawn from above. That sounded epic, and without much consideration we changed our plans. Hopping on the last bus of the day, we bounced our way up the switchback roads, spending the evening waiting at the Fifth Station for the right time to begin our trek. I had both read and been told that the climbing of Fuji-san can take anywhere between 6 and 12 hours, depending on your speed and the number of others climbing. We figured 7 hours would be ample, factoring in a few rests along the way. Slow and steady may win the race, but I have always taken joy in pushing my physical limits and this would be no different.

Or so I thought.

As we waited at the camp we noticed two things. First, the staggering forty-degree heat below us was not so kind as to venture its way up to where we were. Even just a couple thousand meters in elevation made a world of difference. Unprepared as we were, we hadn't packed clothing for a colder climate. Fortunately, the Fifth Station, tourist trap that is, had us covered. A few small shops dotted the slope, enabling us to grab a few last-minute items. I spent a handful of yen buying some gloves — a purchase I was thankful for within minutes of starting our hike — and more snacks. Because I love to snack.

The second thing we discovered was that we were not alone — as white people, that is. While waiting for the right moment to depart we bumped into the other non-Japanese travellers who were heading up the heights this evening. All three of them.

Joining us as we waited were three guys also set on the midnight climb, and together we counted down the hours.

One was a hippie-looking solo traveller from Australia, with flowing curls and a chill disposition. He was your stereotypical Aussie backpacker, his beach bum vibes so weighty that I had to double check he wasn't heading up the mountain in a pair of flip-flops.[29] Our other two companions were BFFs from the UK, an upbeat pair of gents who were always good for a laugh. Since all the Japanese climbers had already departed it was just us foreigners lingering around the buildings of the Fifth Station, taking shelter in the heated restaurant as we watched the hours tick by. Finally, at a time when I would usually be ready for bed, we decked ourselves out and hit the road. It was both reassuring and concerning that they were all unprepared, as well; only one of them had thought to bring a flashlight. Being the only one with a headlamp, I led the way into the pitchy shadow of Mount Fuji.

We kept a solid pace for the first leg, the martian soil crunching under our heavy steps. Energized by our love of adventure, we plodded along at a brisk pace, Christine struggling to keep up due to her lack of tallness. The incline was subtle as we made our way from the station upward, our eyes still adjusting to the early shades of darkness. As we climbed higher, through an emaciated forest and over a bulldozed path, we began to see the environment take shape below us; the lights of all the cities and towns in the distance left a glossy blush across the night sky. Blurry specks and sprawls dotted the landscape below us in all directions, clusters of yellows and whites and oranges, pinpricks of colour resisting the impending dark. A colossal a Lite Brite.

It didn't take long for the beautiful dark to grow cold. Our energy was high and we were all in good spirits, but it was clear that we had miscalculated. This wasn't going to be a walk in the park.

Taking breaks was a necessary part of the climb, not just to rest the legs and lungs but to help acclimatize to the elevation. Japan, being Japan, has allowed the creation of small (and not-so-small) huts along the way so that hikers can stop and grab some refreshment during their climb. Beer, warm noodles, chocolate bars — the bare necessities were all there. My Commonwealth Comrades were keen to break at the first couple stops, shivering in the sooty twilight as they gulped down some steaming ramen. As we paused, our breath huffing and puffing mini clouds of exhaustion, Christine would press on. She was freezing, needing the movement to stay warm against the encroaching winds.

They don't show that on the postcards. You never see postcards or photos of hikers huddling together, sweaty and cold, ducking from the wind as they coddle their soup like it was a newborn baby. Like every international monument or tourist hub, what you see in person isn't always what you see on the post card. Mount Fuji was no different.

As we pressed on, we began to catch up with those who had departed before us. Every few hundred metres, we would pause as the Japanese climbers (many of them double my age) slowly and surely made their way toward the heavens. Decked out in only the best travel gear, the cheerful and dedicated climbers took their hike seriously. In comparison, we looked like a gaggle of *gaijin* completely out of place. Nevertheless, every single hiker made sure to say hello to us.

Every. Single. One.

Dozens of out-of-breath greetings became hundreds, possibly thousands, as we progressed. With a smile, and a bow if we could manage, our well-enunciated *ko-ni-chi-wa* slowly devolved. After the first 50 hikers, it was *k'nichiwaaaa*. A hundred later, it was only *'nichwaa*. Hours into the hike, all we could muster were haphazard and extended *waaas* as we lumbered up the steepening slope. My neck was growing sore from returning the continual half-bows to the ever-polite adventurers on their jingling tramp, my origami spine stiff from the constant folding in polite regard.

I say jingling because a lot of these hardcore hikers had bells attached to their bags. Akin to the little jingly bells you may let a cat play with, or those you hear during a bout of Christmas carolling, perhaps one in every twenty Japanese hikers had them dangling from their bags. My initial thought was that they were something *Shinto* related. Considering that this was one of the Three Holy Mountains of Japan, I figured that was a reasonable assumption, though I didn't feel it appropriate to interrupt any of the climbers mid-hike and pose the question. My assumption, I later found out, was wrong.

The bells were for bears.

Yes, bears.

Every so often, a hiker will find themselves an unwitting victim of the cuddly critters, an unfortunate event that the media will then spin out of whack. Because of this, Japanese hikers rarely leave home without a bear bell. Oddly enough, this precaution is embraced on Mount Fuji, a volcanic wasteland akin to Mordor that is continually hiked and maintained — with bulldozers, no less! — by human beings.

Yeah. Bears.

Bothersome bells aside, our energy was flagging drastically as the climb continued. It never dawned on us, idiots that we are, that climbing a mountain would be incredibly taxing. Braced against the cold, we clung to our stubborn dedication and single-minded focus. They were the foundation of our efforts, more so than any physical stamina or outward preparation. I had convinced myself, pre-Fuji, that *if old people can do it, I can do it*. Perhaps the ageist axiom generally serves, but not here in Japan. The older generation is decidedly hardier than one expects. Tougher than I, anyway.

As the mountain took its toll our conversations dwindled. Our pace drooped to a shuffle. And then a storm rolled in.

A gentle rain misted the slope with sporadic and icy pellets. Rolling clouds rumbled their way ever closer over the vast expanse, blanketing the glassy landscape that slept at our feet. Crisp bolts of lightning, like sharpened forks of white steel, cut the sky, flashing in the distance to the low groan of approaching thunder. Never drawing too near, the flawless spectacle raged for the better part of an hour. Its booming cracks, candid and unrestrained, were the whips that saw us forward. Divine wind at our back, we had no choice but to oblige the midnight tempest. We carried on.

Our pace grew desperate, a slow and steady death march. We had overtaken almost everyone in our desire to find shelter and warmth. Altitude sickness was already upon us, our heads throbbing with each footfall. Nausea was soon to follow, joining our pounding headaches as we reached the final leg. With my eyes half-closed and partially blinded by my scarf, I didn't notice that our group had fractured. Christine and I were left marching onward with one of the UK gents, the other two somewhere behind us, lost in the mists and shadows of the holy mountain. We didn't particularly care at that moment, though, for our goal was near.

It wasn't until I crossed the final threshold that I realized we had made it to the top. It was an anticlimactic finish, the details lost to the night, and we could only gage our arrival by the scanty fragments my headlamp could illuminate. The surprise arrival may have stolen our thunder, but it did little to quash our joy. We had made it!

Unfortunately, we had made it too quickly.

It was just past 3 a.m., which meant we did the entire hike in a mere five hours. At this hour, nothing was open yet — because there are, in fact, buildings on the summit. Vending machines, accommodation, food, a post office, and even Wi-Fi are all now perched upon the sacred mountain. Such are the consequences of modernization.

A thermometer placed at the peak indicated that it was -8 degrees Celsius. Not only had we just climbed to 3776m but we had undergone a 48-degree change in temperature. The snow, infinitesimal flecks of powder white, drifted in swirling patches along the crest. We searched for some sort of refuge as the wind whipped across the volcanic terrain, howling a lycan cry as it pummelled us with fell swoops.

With two hours remaining until the summit buildings opened, we had no choice but to improvise some shelter. Wandering the volcano's peak, we came to some construction equipment. The doors we locked, but we were able to crawl between the treads of one of the bulldozers. Using the plow as a wind shield, we crammed our backpacks against the remaining gaps, blocking as much of the frigid wind as we could. Huddling together, our teeth locked in a continual chatter, we shivered away a handful of minutes. Our reprieve was nonexistent as our hidey-hole did little to shelter us from the elements. Brains battered by the altitude, limbs numb from the cold, we decided — having achieved victory already — that it was time to head down.

We had heard the descent would take three or four hours, and so we clenched our chattering teeth and obliged gravity. With no lights at the summit (and being as underprepared as we were) we failed to realize that there was a separate path for descending Fuji-san. As we foolishly impeded the ascent of all those hikers we had once passed, several tried to explain to us that we were going the wrong way. They did so in Japanese, of course, which was of no use to us. Once again, we were caught in the trap of being polite, exchanging hundreds of *waaaa's* and bows over the course of our hurried decline. Hordes of trekkers, faced etched with quizzical looks, passed us as we stumbled down the mountain in our rushed escape of the cold. We never ran into the other half of our group, crediting their absence to the bears of Mount Fuji.

By dawn, we were approaching the final station, the sunrise lost to the chalky grey of an overcast sky. Returning to the origin of our foolhardy climb, we immediately took shelter in a restaurant graciously open 24-hours, no doubt designed to protect idiot travellers like ourselves from their own uninformed mistakes. We ate, relaxed, and slept like vagabonds along the hard benches as we awaited the appearance of our wayward companions. They eventually arrived, alive and unmauled. They, too, were weary and nauseous, but victorious.

Though they didn't see any bears.

~~~~~

As our bus weaved its way down the switchback roads, a haze of grey shed dull light across the foreign land. The sky hung heavy and low, burdened by the remnants of the previous night's storm. The sun rise was muted, barely visible, and we were left with only the lingering drab of a tired night.

It was perfect.

When in Rome

A Lesson in Anger Management

The hand gestures were nuanced, a language in their own right. They increased in size and speed as the conversation heated; shaking fists became stabbing fingers, the pantomime punctuated by exasperated — and then over-exaggerated — shrugs. Hands blurred, their movements quick and precise. You see, gesticulation in Italy is an art form, a cultural staple that dabbles in the stereotypical. More often than not, it walks hand-in-hand with a raised voice and a healthy dose of passion.

Having walked away the day visiting all the ancient sights one sees in the Eternal City, my partner, her nephew, and I decided to give our flagging feet a break and take the bus back to our budget abode. While I prefer to walk as much as possible when I travel, I figured public transportation would be a well-earned treat after hoofing it around the city. Mapping out a vague course home, we jumped on a half-empty bus, plopping ourselves down in the empty back seats. The semi-shade was refreshing; we were finally free from the clutches of summer. It was mid-August, which in Rome meant it was sweltering. It was also peak travel season in Europe, and the crowded, hectic city was abuzz. We soaked it all in. Gelato here. Gelato there. A few historic sites in between more gelato. By mid-afternoon we were drenched in sweat, our brains swollen from an overdose of history, our bellies from gelato. A bus was necessary.

Sometime during our stop-and-go crawl, a group of men clambered onto the bus. As we began to roll onward, it became clear that one of their friends was left behind. He knocked a few times on the door but the driver was already shifting gears and pushing ahead. Determined, the man started banging on the door with one hand, and then both. He ran beside the bus as it crawled up a hill, shouting and slamming his fists to no avail. His companions on the bus also started yelling at the driver to stop and wait. Voices were raised and raised again and all eyes turned to the commotion. But the driver would take no heed. Indifferent to the disturbance, he shrugged off the verbal onslaught; he was in no mood to alter his schedule. The argument continued for several blocks, hands flailing as it snowballed into a shouting match, the abandoned passenger long since left in our dust. We passengers did our best to mind our own business but it was clear that everyone was watching and listening as the conversation grew heated, even for Italian standards. Nobody else spoke, the artificially-cooled air brimming with an awkward intensity.

As we rolled to the top of a hill, the driver came to an abrupt and unscheduled stop. A few metres away was a collection of police officers — a lot of them, in fact — and our driver decided to park the bus and alert them to the heated situation. He stuck his head out the window, shouting at the cops who stood idle along the roadside. Horns started to honk as we held up traffic, clogging the arteries of an already sluggish city. With no response from the police, the driver was forced to shove his way passed his angry nemeses and march off the bus to get their attention. Crossing traffic, he waved the officers over.

In his furious haste, the driver made an ill-fated mistake: he had leapt from the bus without setting the parking break. We started to roll.

Seriously?

I couldn't help but grin at the absurdity of the situation. Christine immediately looked worried, eyes wide as her brain realized what was happening. It seemed our die was cast.[30]

I watched Christine's knuckles go white as she gripped her seat, the bus starting to creep backward. We picked up speed as our momentum carried us back down the hill, the faces of each passenger etched with varying shades of *oh fuck*. Personally, I wasn't too concerned. There were plenty of cars behind us to impede our descent down the paved hilltop, which meant we couldn't really get too hurt. Everyone else? They would be crushed and mangled...but I was sure we would manage to get by unscathed. I cocked my head around to watch the impending disaster from the large back window. I had a front-row seat as we gathered speed, the rising concerns of other passengers echoing in my ears. Those concerns morphed into full-on shouts and screams as we tipped further down the hill, physics doing what it does best. I watched, jaw dropped, as a woman on a scooter nimbly dodged the bus as it steamrolled her direction. Another rider followed her lead, hoping to swoop past the bus as it cannoned by. He, alas, was too slow. The side of the bus clipped his scooter, sending him spiraling into traffic. While he managed to avoid getting crushed, a nasty gash drew a red line down his exposed calf. We hit the car behind us, jolting in our seats. But we didn't stop.

Our momentum pressed us backward. The car we had just hit ploughed into another. It slammed into another, which slammed into a few more. The pile up stopped our descent long enough for the driver to catch up to us, dive back into the bus, and pull the parking break. He did not, quite understandably, look pleased.

Finally, the policed decided to pay attention.

We hopped off the bus in one piece, shaken but unharmed, our legs disappointed at the all-too-short reprieve. Even in the commotion it was clear that no one was seriously injured, though a curious mob had assembled around the bus. As the police began to take stock of the chaos we simply departed, trudging our way back up the hill from where we had rolled.

By then, the stranded pedestrian who had been abandoned a few stops earlier had caught up with us. The police started to question the driver and his nemeses. Waving hands blurred furious shapes, the conversation an unruly morass encircled by a growing phalanx of curious cops and angry passengers. Pondering our fate as we took in the chaotic scene, it was clear what we had to do next: it was time for more gelato.

This time, though, we'd skip the bus.

Racism 101

A Lesson in Assumptions

What madness it is in your expecting evil before it arrives!
~ Seneca the Younger

In case it isn't obvious this far in, I'm not a resort kind of guy. Sure, I like chilling on the beach every now and then, and relaxing in a king-sized bed is an occasional treat...but I also like to wander, to mingle with the places I go. I like to test the cultural waters and see what lingers beneath the surface. Beyond the initial expectations. You are hard pressed to do that at a resort because a resort is, in a way, a voluntary prison. A luxurious prison, but a prison nonetheless. You get a room, you get food, you get planned outdoor activities, and you get lots of free time to just do nothing. It's a walled community, separate from the country itself, that sanitizes the locale and presents a watered-down version of it.

And sometimes that's ok.

Sometimes we need that escape, to pamper ourselves, to have some time to decompress. I get that. But that's the difference between a *vacation* and *travel*. One is an escape. The other is a challenge.

I'm fortunate in that I don't have anything I feel the need to escape from, which is perhaps partly why "vacations" aren't the kind of trip that resonates with me; I'll take rustic depth over shallow luxury eight days a week. My dad, however, loves a good resort. Hardly the intrepid backpacker, he feels at home there; he loves planning new routines in a place where the weather is more cooperative than that of Canada. Give him a consistent 30-degrees Celsius and a decent gym and he will be content for a lifetime. That's why, after popping down to visit a few resorts in the Caribbean and Mexico, he bought himself a timeshare. And a swank one at that.

For my 25th birthday, now many moons ago, my dad and stepmom were kind enough to offer me the use of their timeshare for a week. Prison or not, a week of luxurious down time in Puerto Vallarta was hardly the worst of things. I hastily rounded up some friends, booked my ticket, and headed down to Mexico for some fun in el sun.

Now, I read the news every day. I probably shouldn't, but I like to stay current on all the horrible shit that is happening in this here world. An avid reader of both corporate and alternative news media, I was vaguely versed in all the corruption and ill-happenings that had been going on in Mexico. While I am fully aware of the inherent hyperbole of the modern media machine, I was nevertheless a tad wary of getting too far off the beaten track. Awareness of these things is good when you travel, as you need to keep safe wherever you go. The first step to staying safe is being aware of your surroundings. While I was far more likely to get mugged back home in Toronto, I had a lingering shadow of ignorant skepticism looming over me as I headed south.

With the hope of avoiding some dreaded bank fees, I had taken a bunch of cash with me before I left. Zipped in into a hidden pocket of my backpack, I considered it safe and sound. I had been around the travel block by this point and was familiar with how to not get pick-pocketed (Hint: use common sense). Our flights south were uneventful — which is just how I like my flights — and we landed in Mexico without issue. As we made our way out of the airport and into the sticky heat I flipped my backpack over to grab some cash for our shuttle...and I noticed it was open. And not just a little, either — the whole back pouch was open. That would be, of course, where I had my "secret" wad of cash.

FUCK.

In the back of mind, for but the briefest flash of a moment, I thought:

OF COURSE I GOT ROBBED! I'M IN MEXICO!

I frantically double checked my bag, heart racing. I played through the past few minutes, crawling over my memory in search of some suspicious clue. *Fuck fuck fuck fuck fuck.* I could feel my face getting red, the flush of embarrassed anger tip-toeing down my neck. I checked my pockets, my coat, my wallet. I tore through my backpack, checking every crevasse. *Just my fucking luck!* Tearing open a zipper I came to the hidden pouch where, lo and behold, my money was safely located.

BECAUSE I'M AN IDIOT!

I had merely forgotten it was hidden in the compartment *underneath* the exposed pocket, leaving it completely safe and sound. I stopped in my tracks, zipping up all the pockets and pouches as I puffed an incredulous sigh of relief.

Jumping into our shuttle, I was still a bit dazed and distraught. Caught up in my own self-analyzing, I merely mumbled my way through the small talk with our taxi driver. We weaved through the hectic Mexican traffic, where it seemed the rules of the road were more guidelines than anything else. The heat was a welcome change from frigid Canada, though after my near heart attack I was already dotted with sweat. As we rolled to a stop near our uncomfortably fancy resort, I passed the driver a bill in exchange for the ride and helping with the luggage. Lost analyzing the implicit racism of my earlier thoughts, I miscalculated the amount of pesos I should have tipped. Setting down the last of our backpacks, he glanced awkwardly at the bill in his hand.

"Sir, is this tip just from you or is it from everyone?"

Distracted, I barely looked up, certain my math was socially acceptable.

"It's from all of us — thanks for your help!"

My thanks was genuine, though I had failed to realize that I had just tipped him a buck when it should have been closer to $10.

"Well sir, if this is all you can tip then please keep it. You must need it more than I do."

With a sarcastic smile, he set the crumpled bill on my friend's suitcase, hopped back in the shuttle, and drove away. Confused, I said nothing. It was then, double checking my math, that I realized I was a total fuck up.

I had just insulted someone because I was too busy thinking about what I had *just* been thinking about: that my immediate reaction to arriving in a country full of non-white people was to blame them for robbing me.

I had flash backs to the town where I grew up, a place where I could count the number of non-white residents on one hand. *Was I racist?* Not in a cross-burning, KKK kind of way, but perhaps something more subtle? I was genuinely distraught, though I kept the whole thing to myself, mulling over my thoughts and actions as I pondered the privilege of being white.

Now, we can't really help what we think. We *can* control what we say and do (and we can improve our basic math skills) but controlling what we think proves next to impossible. I have ridiculous thoughts pretty much all the time. Some are benign, like my desire for a crunchy peanut butter that spreads smoothly BUT THEN becomes crunchy once more. Others are more insidious, fed by the institutionalized biases ingrained in our societies.

It is those thoughts, the harmful, subversive ones, that we should actively strive to smother. They can be hard to notice, but if you let shit like that take root than you are going to have some serious problems when they intellectually blossom in the future. However, if you can manage to let those thoughts float by like the little potentially-racist clouds they sometimes are, then they dissipate into the ether of your weird little head. Unfortunately, many of us from "the West" have all inherited bits and pieces of the institutional racism that surrounds us. It is something we digest, tacitly or otherwise, and it permeates us all to varying degrees, which is a low down dirty shame. People all around the world in all sorts of wonderful places get a bad rap thanks to our preconceived notions and expectations about who they are and what their values are in relation to ours. We are judging them before we even hop on a plane, train or automobile — and that isn't fair. As travellers, we need to keep an open mind and an open heart. That doesn't mean be careless, but it doesn't mean you get to be an ignorant ass either.

In the end, we are all just people trying to get by. We need to check our fears at the door and waltz into the world with pocketful of compassion and a fistful of wisdom. Do that, and you'll be surprised how un-scary this little planet of ours really is.

~~~~~

Nothing bad actually happened to me on that trip, and to this day the only times I've been robbed have been in Canada and Sweden. And you don't get much whiter than those places.

and in every falling snow flake
lived one thousand years of summer,
bright and burning
and in that bright and burning,
the coldest fields clung to life
a stubborn winter, holding on

Christopher Kevin Oldfield

Done to the Top

A Lesson in Positive Thinking

Hakuna Matata

I could hear the ravens. They circled about the camp, diving low to weave between our weather-worn tents. The *whoosh-whoosh* of their jet-black wings glided over the din of the porters and their rowdy conversations. Their shadows were fleeting, ghosts on the stone and canvas. As they swooped low, dancing about, the gusts of wind from their wings pressed into my tent with an audible thud. The birds had been with us since day three of our journey, circling in as we shuffled along the windswept trail toward the forebodingly-named Lava Tower.

At lunch, they would perch themselves nearby, hopping about, hoping for scraps. We would stare at one another, heads cocked in mirrored interest. They had sinister faces, beaks curved in a vicious grin, a Glasgow Smile bestowed by evolution. Beady eyes watched me from the rocks above, each bird marked by a white splotch of colour at the base of its neck. Sprawled out on the cold stone of the mountain, hiding from a bitter wind, I pondered why they had evolved with such a pattern. The stark black and speckled white reminded me of war paint, a warning that I was no longer in familiar territory. This was their mountain.

This was Kilimanjaro.

Sitting there, on the frost-bound slopes, we were in their element. They watched us indifferently, waiting to feast on our leftovers: chicken bones and sandwich crusts and, should the mountain win the day, the marrow of our very bones.

I had decided to climb Kilimanjaro — the tallest free-standing mountain in the world — on something of a whim. I was in Kenya visiting my sister and we figured, *"Well, we're in the neighbourhood..."* With zero training, and lacking most of the basic supplies, we made our way to Tanzania via a cramped and hastily driven bus, found ourselves some guides, and began what I consider one of the most challenging things I've ever done.[31]

Fortunately for us, this was not an endeavour we could undertake alone. Leading us into the fray were two guides and a team of porters whom we had heard would get us to the top come hell or high water. Mike, a young local in his late twenties, was our head guide. He was soft spoken and tall, pushing a few inches over six feet. His face was round and soft, chipmunk-like, and often framed by a purple bandana that kept the sun and wind at bay. His deep brown eyes were equal parts relaxed and attentive. He spoke almost perfect English, a qualification that rose him from the backbreaking ranks of the *porters* — the men who hauled our gear up the mountain for a meagre wage — and into a better payed and more respected position of *guide*. While he was young, he was nevertheless decidedly experienced: he had been up the mountain well over 100 times. His first summit occurred when he was only 18, and it was as a porter. Strapped to forty pounds of gear, he carried his scrawny self up and down the mountain. No trial run. No training. Just *up*.

His assistant was an older man from his village, a man he had known since childhood. Just shy of 60 years old, Jack had trudged his way up Kilimanjaro well over 300 times over the past fifteen years. Not surprisingly, his gait was nonchalant, his pace slow and steady, as if the mountain couldn't resist his patient onslaught. His skin was smooth, wrinkles held at bay by the positive vibes that emanated from his carefree attitude. His English was broken, leaving him grasping at the right words as he worked to keep us informed during the climb. What he lacked in linguistic quantity he made up for in quality, harnessing the power of memorable catchphrases to keep us all in good spirits.

As we progressed up the mountain we came to realize that, more than any training, more than any awesome gear, there was one critical element you needed on Kilimanjaro: a positive attitude. That fact was hammered home directly by Mike, who always reminded us to relax and enjoy the trip, to focus on each day as it came. It was also hardwired into the very essence of Jack, who I spent most of my time with. His philosophy — on the mountain, on life — was summed up in his clichéd, but heartfelt, catchphrase response to any situation:

No problem.

No worries.

Piece of cake.

Easy peasy.

Hakuna Matata.

With these five phrases, Jack could address any problem; and it was, quite literally, the extent of his English. Truth be told, it was all you really needed. Have to pee? *No worries.* Need a break for water? *No problem.* Struggling to climb a mountain almost 6,000 metres tall? *Piece of cake.*

Our battleground was the Lemosho route, a winding trail we would call home for seven days. While it was more scenic than the popular Machame route, it also had a lower success rate. Our odds of making it to the top were sitting pretty at around 75%. I had shoved my chips all in for worse odds than that, so I wasn't overly concerned. The most common factors that hindered hikers were altitude sickness and the weather. I made sure to pack some pills for the altitude, leaving our fate in the fickle hands of the elements.

This is not to say the hike wasn't demanding — it most certainly was. The final day involved almost 16 hours of trekking, including a 7-hour summit which began at midnight. Kilimanjaro is no Everest, but it is definitely no walk in the park, either. It was never far from my mind that one wrong step could send you home bloodied. Between the jagged rocks and sheer cliff faces, an injury didn't seem unlikely. A handful of people actually die on the mountain every year, a statistic which includes a friend of my boss. This was, to be clear, no afternoon stroll.

Nothing hit that home more than the Barranco Wall.

On day four of my hike I encountered the wall: 250 meters of solid rock, craggy and hungry. It was a daunting cliff face and would require a fistful of diligence and a pinch of luck. Fortunately, climbers don't need to vertically ascend the wall but rather slink their way along the slope on a diagonal, all while doing their level best to avoid tumbling to their death. It was a stop-and-go ascent, the kind that makes you second-guess the very reasons why you're on the mountain. There were sections that required us to hug the wall and shimmy along a narrow ledge, precisely the kind of ledge you'd avoid on an average day. There was no safety line, either, just a hope and a prayer that you would make it. Another section required us to leap — a literal leap of faith — over a precarious gap in the path. A miscalculation would send us into the abyss if we failed. The obstacles on the Barranco Wall were daring enough to give most people pause, to get the blood flowing, adrenaline pumping.

Of course, any time I mentioned the challenge to our hearty

guides I was met with a smile and a pat on the back from Jackson. *Hakuna Matata*, he would say. *No problem*, he would say. By then, of course, all you could do was smile and repeat the phrase, willing yourself to stay positive as you shrugged off the challenge. Though as many climbers learned that day, it's hard to hold on with your fingers crossed.

It was the perfect reminder that, more than anything, Kilimanjaro was a mental battle. And that travel, too, was a risk in and of itself. But a sharp mind and a positive attitude will always win the day; they will take you infinitely farther than any plane ticket evert could.

As my beloved partner always says, "You gotta risk it for the biscuit."

~ ~ ~ ~ ~

As we prepped for the final day, I moseyed over to our guides to ask why we were summiting at night, why we had to start the hike to the top at midnight. Call me crazy, but hiking the during the day seemed infinitely more enjoyable than a blind death march to the top. I had done a midnight hike before, if you recall, and it wasn't the most endearing experience. Cupping a steaming mug of black coffee, Mike scooped a few spoonsfuls of sugar and dropped them into his drink before replying, his spoon clinking against the metal in slow repetition.

"Because at night, you cannot see the top. You cannot see how far you must go."

He looked to the mountain, almost as if they were in conversation, as if he were listening to a whisper I couldn't hear. And they he turned to me directly, his brown eyes staring into mine.

"And because you cannot see, my friend, you cannot quit."

And he was right.

Without a visual reference, you really had no idea how far you had to go. You could ask your guide, but he would lie, knowing it would lull you into pressing on (which is precisely what Mike did). Hiking seven hours at a pace that covers only half a foot with every step is tedious; it's a mental battle as much as it is a physical one. People turn back mere hours from the summit, their body and mind folding to the pressure, their hopes dashed to feed the ravens. I witnessed hikers collapse from the exertion, from the altitude, crumpled and exhausted as they huffed and puffed warm air into the frigid atmosphere. Those still on their feet clawed forward, shivering in the dark as the temperature slipped to a desperate -20 Celsius. A sparse line of headlamps dotted the mountainside, like faded Christmas lights strung up without a plan. Headaches spread, lungs grew weary, extremities went numb. I was wearing 5 layers on my torso and 4 on my legs, somehow both sweating and freezing as I mindlessly dragged my feet onward and upward. All I could do was press on, every moment a new opportunity to give in, to give up. Step by step, it was battle. A test.

Right foot. *Piece of cake.*

Left foot. *Hakuna Matata.*

Step by step. *No problem.*

I worked a mantra into my pace, an old Buddhist tune I picked up years ago from one of Thich Nhat Hanh's books.

I have arrived. I am home

In the here. In the now

I am solid. I am free

In the ultimate I dwell.

Every step, a breath. Every step, part of the mantra. Head low, eyes on my feet. I turned my headlamp off, my eyes well-adjusted to the pre-dawn shadow. Quitting wasn't an option. Victory or death. *Easy Peasy.*[32]

By the time, we were nearing the summit, dawn was stretching her hungry talons over the horizon. My throat was parched, my water bottle long since frozen. But the summit was near, within sight. I had passed 9 different groups as I pushed forward, each left to follow in my footsteps as I willed myself beyond the clouds. The sky was bleeding purple, a bruise of light stretching out before me. My face was cold, my fingers tingling and bloodless. Slender slices of orange stabbed into the murky blues and deepening purples of the sunrise, the clouds well below us, kneeling to our might. I stared at the horizon until my eyes hurt, until they watered tears that froze against my skin. It was a sunrise etched onto my heart, one I'll carry with me for the rest of my days.

I had made it to the Roof of Africa.

Feet planted, lungs brimming, I tasted life on top of a continent. For but a moment, I was the tallest person in Africa; no one with their feet on the ground was closer to the heavens than myself. Casting my bloodshot eyes to the endless horizon, I felt so powerful, so limitless. And yet so insignificant, a beat-up pebble on a mountain that will live forever. I savored the sensation as long as I could. It was a feeling I had had before, one I'm sure I'll have again. *Somewhere.* It's no doubt one you've felt, too. In your heart, in your gut. It hits you like a frozen moment, like a cosmic déjà vu. That feeling of being everything and nothing. It's a universal experience, It think, a profound juxtaposition that binds us all together.

It's the feeling of being human.

It hit me at 20,000 feet above sea level, where the air was razor thin and desperately cold. I couldn't bring myself to take my gloves off for more than a moment to snap some pictures, proof I had overcome the mountain, and myself. Proof I was nothing and everything. I fumbled with the camera, my fingers fat and red, stiff and swollen from the altitude and from the meds I had taken to avoid getting nauseous. A side-effect of victory.

With a second wind clawing in my ribcage and an icy wind battering my skin, I headed back down. *No problem.*

The next day I found my weary self back at the outfitters. I was given a certificate proving I had made it to the summit. I was also given a t-shirt. On the back of the shirt, it listed the altitude of Kilimanjaro — 5,895 meters — and celebrated my victory in broken English:

DONE TO THE TOP!

Just the Tip

That was the Instagram version, the polished and triumphant story that aims to inspire. It's the bikini and sunhat pic, the generic photo with carpe diem ejaculated all over it. Anyone who travels knows that, while these stories aren't inherently shallow, they also don't paint the most complete picture. Enter Part Two.

"How much cash do you have, again?"

It was my sister, and she asked just as I was tallying a wad of once-crisp Tanzanian shillings I had pulled from my backpack. I lost count as she spoke, unenthusiastically shuffling the bills back into a pile before starting over.

For the past week, we'd been focused purely on surviving. As we limped our way back down to base camp, our priorities began to shift. "Survival" was steadily losing ground to the practicalities of adventure, such as "paying for our trip" and "the need to bathe." Addressing said practicalities, we somehow found ourselves crotch deep in a situation that was only going to get more awkward as we lost altitude. Counting our cash, it seemed we didn't have the money we needed for tipping our guides. Or, rather, for tipping the guides the amount they *wanted* to be tipped...

While you can scroll through Instagram and binge on heavily-edited pictures of Kili, what you won't find in the brochure is the whole clusterfuck that is tipping your guides.

Tipping your team — the porters, guides, cooks, and everyone else on your crew — is expected after your climb. It's a built-in mechanism to show your appreciation...whether you want to or not. To make things "easier" there are suggested rates for each team member, based on what they do. *Porters get between X-Y each day, cooks between Y-Z each day,* etc. Not being a totally idiot, I checked into all of this before we embarked on our hike and made sure to have some cash on hand for the inevitable exchange. The internet — God bless it's morally-bankrupt soul — gave me some approximate guidelines, and those corresponded with what some friends had told me, as well. All seemed kosher on the mountainside.

Until Mike came to chat with us.

He stepped into our tent as my sister and I were huddled over our tea in full recovery mode. He looked tired, stooped from the previous night's gung-ho death march to the summit. His eyes were red, but his voice remained upbeat and friendly. Having just rolled our way down from the peak, we were not in much of a mood for anything but rest. Battered and exhausted, we mustered up the energy to play social. Seeing as it was him who got us to the top, we didn't want to kick up a fuss.

In his soft voice, he mentioned the tips, probing to see the extent of our knowledge. Too tired to speak, we just played dumb and allowed him to coast through his spiel.

"Have you been told about the tipping process?"

I gave a half-hearted shrug.

"We have some idea."

Clearly, what my idea was and what Mike's was were two oh-so-very different things. I had planned to tip around $300. That roughly worked out to about 15% of the cost my trip. It was about what I had read online, too, so it seemed reasonable. I expected to unceremoniously toss it in an envelope, hand it to my guides, and be on my way. What I didn't know was that it wouldn't be so simple.

Mike rattled off his suggested numbers and I mentally followed along. Dancing around the basic math, his total came to $1,000 USD, or just under 50% of the cost of our trip. Now, I don't know about you but where I come from a 50% tip usually involves way more hand jobs or high fives.

But seriously, a 50% tip? It was a far cry from the $300 I had budgeted. Something was rotten in the state of Denmark...

Now, don't get me wrong, these guys absolutely deserved to be fairly compensated for their work. They sweat and bleed so that privileged assholes like me can sit pretty on top of a mountain and write haikus. They are the real heroes here, and they absolutely should be making a fair, livable wage. That wage should enable them to get by without awkwardly prodding their patrons for tips. As the head guide, Mike had to look out for his team, and I respect that. I'd do the same if the situation was reversed.[33]

But $1,000? Fuck.

Even if I wanted to fork over that much cash, it was impossible. I was limited to a withdrawal of $300 per day via the ATM's here, and that was assuming they would accept my card (which wasn't always the case, I discovered). I exchanged a sidelong glance with my sister as Mike left, herself well aware of the financial hand grenade he had lobbed into our tent. We didn't have much time to worry, though, because we were immediately invited outside for an impromptu performance.

As we learned then and there, it was customary for each team to sing a song for their climbers at the end of the trek, a traditional conclusion to the adventure. We heard the fading reverie of other groups as their own songs lingered in the breezeless air. Our own crew, over a dozen strong, had gathered around their tents as we approached, bunched together to form a rag-tag chorus of scrawny superheroes who ate mountains for breakfast. They belted out a catchy tune, and it would have been an immersive experience if it wasn't for the nagging feeling in my gut that they didn't want to be singing. They were, quite literally, singing for their supper and it didn't sit right. I plastered a smile to my face, tapping my toe to the rhythm as the song rolled along, echoing against the stone and drifting off into hills. This was the whoring of culture and it was clear none of us were enjoying it.

Afterward, Mike gave a short speech to thank us and we in turn genuinely applauded them for their efforts. There was no doubt in my mind that we wouldn't have made it without a reliable crew. Catching Mike's eyes, he leaned in toward us.

"…and do you want to say something about the tips?"

It was a leading question, the kind that leads you into oncoming traffic.

"Oh, right. Um. So…we will be taking care of the tips when

we get back to the office."

I let an awkward pause flash in the conversational pan before continuing.

"We didn't want to bring all that money on the mountain. In case it...got wet or whatever."

If my response was a text message I would have ended with a shrug emoji followed by the smiling face with cold sweat. Classic but understated. Unfortunately, all the porters had flip phones so I doubt my emoji choice would have translated, anyway.

So much for bridging cultures.

We bounced our way back to the office over dirt roads more pot-holed than they were flat, 15 people packed into a 12-person van with no functioning seatbelts. Dying on the drive back would have been hilariously ironic but I was too tired to care. We all smelled terrible — the stale and unwashed scent of victory — and were excited to get somewhere with a real bed and a working shower and, if we were extra lucky, hot water.

But first we had to hand out the tips. Those fucking tips.

After a hearty congratulation and the issuing of our DONE TO THE TOP shirts, we asked our outfitter about the tipping amount, hoping for a sober second opinion.

"It's just what you can afford, something extra, to thank them."

He, too, went over the numbers, inching his way just shy of $1,000 only to then reiterate that, "It's whatever you can afford, what seems fair."

It was a sneaky card to play. What "seems fair?" These guys

just hauled ass up a mountain, carrying my gear and making sure I could jizz Instagram magic once I returned to the land of Wi-Fi. They were heroes, unequivocally. They worked harder than most people back home and paying them accordingly is what "seems fair."

But how much of that is my job? Why does the patron have to pay the employee? Isn't that the boss' job? Don't get me wrong, a tip for going above and beyond is fine by me...but a tip that is more or less their salary? Seems more sketchy than fair if you ask me.

We shuffled out the door and into a light rain to search for an ATM. My sister only had $100 on hand, a fry cry from the $300 she needed (or the $1,000 Mike was hoping for). One after another, they declined our cards, the staff at each bank less than helpful with our predicament. Eventually, we were able to make a quick withdrawal — a mere $300 — before returning to chit chat with our team. It was a gut-wrenchingly forced conversation, one imposed by our outfitter. The crew stuck around out of obligation, patiently waiting for their tips and counting down the moments until they could go home to their families. We were counting down the moments until we could go to our two-star hotel and shower off the past week's worth of sweat and stink and dirt. Our only impediment was the small talk that stood between us, a social morass no one was in the mood for.

As the conversation stalled, I started working on the tip list. Stuffing a fistful of crumpled bills into an envelope, I was told, is not how you hand over the tips. It's expected that you make a list for the tip amounts for each individual and then call out the numbers publically, a financial roll call, so that everyone knows what they get and there are no surprises.

There was no way in hell I was doing that.

Sipping on a well-earned, ice-cold Fanta, I scribbled each

position onto the paper. *Guide. Assistant guide. Cook. Toilet Engineer. Waiter. Porter.* I thought about writing their names but I didn't know them all and, quite frankly, couldn't spell half of them. Beside each position, I wrote the tip amount, making clear the break down. Guides got the most, porters got the least. Everyone else was in between. I followed the estimates I had read online, making sure it was clear who was getting what. I folded the paper around the thick tower of bills and slid it to Mike, thanking him once again. I expected he would tuck it away for later but he unfolded the paper immediately and eyed the numbers.

I could sense an immediate wave of disappointment. I could see it in those big, glossy brown eyes of his. He adjusted his bandana, eyes remaining low, lips tight. Sipping his beer, Jack glanced at the numbers but couldn't have cared less.

No worries.

As for me, I felt terrible. These guys truly deserved to be paid well, but I mentally reaffirmed my position: yes, they deserved more but a 15% tip is fair. *Employers are responsible for their employees, not the customers.* And while I was much better off financially than these guys, a surprise 35% increase in price wasn't something I felt was fair nor affordable.

After a few sporadic final handshakes, we slinked away from the scene, crawling into a taxi that would shuttle us back to normalcy. It was a sour note to end on, having just clawed our way to the Roof of Africa. A disappointing denouement.

Fortunately for us, there were other mountains to climb.

when the crows pick at my bones
pecking at the scraps of my tendons and marrow
they will know
I conquered mountains

One Hand Clapping

Another Lesson in Cause and Effect

Okayama, Japan. A city nestled between Hiroshima and Kobe on the main island of Honshu, it's there where I've was living my monken life at a Zen Buddhist monastery. Built at the foot of a forested mountain, the monastic grounds were semi-engulfed by the encroaching city. Within a 5-minute walk you could reach a 24-hour grocery store, an elementary school, and if you walked another 5 minutes, a 24-hour casino. The last bastion of privacy came from the surrounding suburban houses that kept the urban sprawl at bay, though every so often the whirling blades of helicopters or distant pitch of sirens could still be heard in the sharpened silence of the meditation hall.

Adjusting to monastic life, understandably, took some time. The schedule was rigorous, involving 8-15 hours of meditation per day. Our wake-up call would rouse us at 3:30 a.m., and lights out was anywhere between 9 and 11 p.m. A day or two each month we were permitted to sleep in until 6 a.m. Never in my life had 6 a.m. felt so luxurious.

The taxing schedule was precisely why I chose that monastery. I wanted to dig in, to dig deep. I wanted to see who I was, beyond all distractions and excuses. When you sit still you are forced to confront the reality of the moment; you cannot escape yourself. It is there, on the cushion, where your life catches up to you.

Steadily, I adjusted to the spartan meals eaten in silence, to the daily chores of raking sand and sweeping *tatami* (and, if you recall, the less-regular tasks of emptying septic tanks). I also adjusted to the penetrating cold of a wintery Japan. Monasteries, of course, don't have heating. Shivering yourself to near death, I am told, builds character.[34]

To stave off the cold we drank copious amounts of tea, and often just glasses of flavourless hot water when we were desperate. The temperature hovered around zero degrees, and the paper-thin walls did little to insulate. Our razor-shaved heads and bare feet were invitations to the biting chill, my skin a soft hue of icy blue wherever it wasn't swollen red from the chilblains. Earlier in the week, when I asked a senior monk how he dealt with the physical hardship (himself battling a cold at the time) he merely shrugged and said, "It's only my body." Those words stuck with me, and while my teeth chattered hard enough to tire my jaw, I worked to accept my conditions.

On one night in particular, however, those conditions became troublesome.

We were in the middle of *sanzen*, a period of meditation where, one by one, we go and meet with the *Roshi*.[35] It is a very intimate exchange, a fleeting period where the teacher may probe the mind of the student and where the student may demonstrate his understanding, his presence. These exchanges are where the semi-cliché Zen phrases (called *koans*) are encountered. *What is the sound of one hand clapping? What did you look like before your grandmother was born? When you can do nothing, what can you do?* These are the fuel to the fires of Zen, mental whetstones to sharpen one's focus.

It was in the evening of one late-November day when I found my own focus in dire straits. The reason? I needed to use the facilities.

Kneeling on a thin pillow, I was sharpening my own concentration as I worked to ignore my bodily cues. My hand was wrapped around a smooth, small baton, waiting for my invitation to *sanzen*. Within moments, I would hear a jingling bell from across the garden, the metallic rattling my signal to make my way into the serene, candle-lit quarters of the *Roshi* for my interview. But Lord, did I ever have to use the bathroom...and not just to drain all that hot tea water, either. Leaning over the gong that I would soon leave ringing, my folded body pressed on my guts, inching the numerous clumps of tofu and sticky rice further down my intestines.

Enlightenment is a funny thing when you have to take a shit.

I heard the call. From across the pond came the ringing of the bell, like a metal jar full of tiny cymbals all crashing and vibrating. I slammed the gong once, paused for a breath, and then hit it again. It cut into the night, its echo lingering in the crafted silence. I pressed my fingers into the dry *tatami*, pushing myself upward as my knees cracked and bent back to life. The blood rushed downward to my half-numb feet as I bowed, my tingling toes a mere nuisance as my intestines were once more folded like origami. I made my way to the teacher in concentrated steps. Desperate steps. Working to keep my body in check, I employed an age-old meditation trick: I half-tightened my anal sphincter. The old masters say it raises the *chi* so you become less tired and more aware. It's also helpful when you need to bow and walk and bow some more and don't want to shit your flowing robes.

Will he know I have to take a shit? Can Zen masters sense that?

When my brief interview was over, I made my way back to the meditation hall, bowing to another monk as he passed by. My flip-flops *flopping* on the old stone path was the only sound that I could hear. The winding route made its way through perfectly-raked sand gardens, illuminated by the bright white of a clear moon. Moss-covered trees cast leaning shadows in the dull light, like bony fingers reaching to pluck the stars from blue-black sky. They stood witness to a thousand generations of wisdom and clarity and peace…and now, to me clenching my ass as I waddled by, trying my darndest to focus on the cosmic oneness of all things. I was cold to the bone, so cold it hurt, but I was strangely content. I filled my lungs with the icy air as I softly padded my way to the meditation hall, both consciously and unconsciously trying not to shit and piss myself as I basked in the moment.

Pulling me from my task was the sudden flash of a light snapping on. I stopped in my tracks, squinting toward the beams of artificial illumination that leaked from a nearby doorframe. My prayers had been answered: the guest washroom! Praise Buddha, etc.

Tucked away beside the monastery kitchen was an old wooden stall with all the basic amenities one needs. Having never used it, its very existence had slipped my mind as I focused on my intestinal enlightenment. I waited for the current occupant to complete their task, lurking in the shadows nearby. I watched the night, eyes adjusting to the faint glow of the moon and stars, ears hearing only the sound of my heartbeat. The city was nonexistent; it was so still, so dark. Occasionally, distant shouts and growls would pierce the night air in traditional Rinzai fashion.[36] The booming voice of my teacher would reply, and then the silence would blanket us all once more.

HWhhhaaahhhshhhhhhhhhh

The majestic sound of a toilet flushing. The trickling of tap water. The slow grind of wood on wood as the hand-made lock turned and the door creaked open. The flash of light from a 40-watt bulb, briefly obscured by a nun shuffling out of the stall and back into the night.

It was my time to shine. And it would be a photo finish.

I stepped into the small hut, barely 2 square meters in size. In it was a basic sink and a squat toilet with decidedly-inadequate lighting.

It would do.

I hiked up my robes and *hakama*, the traditional Japanese skirt that makes using any sort of toilet something of a coin toss. I bundled what I could underneath my armpits in a vain attempt to not stain my precious garments as I squatted above the shining porcelain. This was my first go at using a squat toilet, as the monastery was kind enough to install western toilets in the meditation hall. While inexperienced, I was familiar with the general concept and so I dove in. Within moments my knees were aching, my toes tensed and digging into the cheap plastic of my sandals. It was awkward and fumbly, but I was managing. With one hand holding my robes and the other propping myself up against the wall, I began to go to work.

Now, I'd like you to imagine something for a moment. Picture a hose, say, a faded-green garden hose with a bright orange adjustable nozzle. If you were to spray said hose against a wall and stand, say, ten feet away you would stay dry. The water would hit the wall and splash back but none would really make it ten feet, thanks to physics or whatever. If you instead stood, say, one foot away, what would happen? Chances are you would be sprinkled by some splash back, right? The water would slam into the wall with enough force to reach you. This is cause and effect. Physics. Karma. Samsara, even. Call it what you will.

Unfortunately, I was that garden hose. As for the wall, it was a mere 4 inches below me. Cue the splash back.

I found myself an immediate victim of cause and effect in the karmic form of my own piss spraying against my thighs, hand, feet, and robes. Not wanting to be doused in the effects of my cause, I aimed my stream further downward and backward, shrugging up my robes as I tried to maintain balance like the beautiful human that I am. Problem solved: no more splash back.

And then I felt something. Something...odd.

As I pointed my...*whatever-the-Japanese-word-for-dick-is* backward I had pushed it too far. Beyond the neutral zone and into the realm of where shit happens. Literally. And so, in what can only be summarized as a majestic moment in my adult life, I had shit on my own dick.

In a pristine moment of Zen-like clarity I came to understand the sound of one hand clapping. I could hear it, serenading the cosmos, echoing through my very being. It was a mocking slow clap, barely audible above the sound of my rolling eyes and stifled chuckle.

Being the monastic type, I didn't bother getting annoyed. *Of course* I would shit on my dick at some point in life — that's just how the universe works. As the first tenet of Buddhism reminds us: *life involves suffering*. Occasionally that suffering is weird and awkward and involves your own fecal matter. As my wise co-monk had said earlier, "It's only my body."

Within a few hurried moments my bodily fluids — both liquid and solid — had completed their evacuation. I assessed the damage and cleaned up as best I could, removing my entire robe and the kimono under it, as well as my *hakama*. Left in just an undershirt and long johns, I shivered my way in through the shady one-ply clean up, never to tell anyone about what had happened.

But Buddha knew, that fat laughing bastard. And now so do you. *Gassho.*

The Flying Dutchman

A Lesson in Walking Fast and Staying Sober

Christine shakes me awake. I have finally fallen asleep to the *pitter-patter* of gentle rain and soft, rolling thunder, courtesy of an app on my outdated iPhone. A t-shirt is draped loosely over my face, blocking every beam of wayward light that threatens to keep me from my beauty rest. As a tragically soft sleeper, these are necessary steps whenever I sleep in a hostel…and even then, I barely manage more than a few hours of shut eye. Between creaking bunks, snoring comrades, and a general lack of pitch-black darkness, sleep is often beyond my feeble grasp.

Jolted by another elbow from Christine, I wake. I can't help but feel disappointed that my rest was so short, but I immediately perk up as she whispers in my ear.

"The police are here."

Rubbing the sleep from my eyes, it takes me a moment to remember where, precisely, *here* is. We're in Spain on the Camino, and every day brings a new town or village to remember. Waking in the middle of the night, those foreign names and places are all a jumble in my head. One eventually bubbles to the surface: Najera. Nájera? Najèra? I stop caring almost immediately.

We've bunked up in the municipal *albergue*. It's a 90-bed dorm room, the largest I think I have ever stayed in. After a few hours of percolating it smells of ripe sweat and tired feet, the air thick and stuffy and dry. I fumble for my phone, leaning up on my elbows as my brain lazily sputters into consciousness. It's 12:34 a.m. and the lights are on. I can only assume this isn't a social call.

I glance toward the scene unfolding beside me, where the Spanish police are quietly talking with a friendly Dutchman one bunk over. He is a bearded giant who I overheard had walked all the way from the Netherlands. Not only has he crossed the continent, though, he has allegedly done it with but a single blister. Standing tall at around six and a half feet, he is a hiking fiend and I already admire the man and his impressive accomplishment. Christine and I are nine days into our Camino and her feet are a disaster. She is tallying a dozen blisters that leave her feet a painful (and let's be honest, disgusting) mess. How the Dutchman has fared so well is nothing short of miraculous.

The police and the bearded giant engage in a muffled conversation as we all look on in silence. Sporadic snores pipe up here and there, proof that some people truly can sleep through anything. By the time I've rubbed the sleep from my eyes and regained some semblance of focus, the Dutchman is getting to his feet. He towers over the hunched officers beside him, his broad shoulders spanning the aisle between bunks. As he strides toward the lobby, flanked by the two officers, a woman in a neighbouring bunk shoots him a snide remark. I don't catch the words, but it's a subtle clue that sheds some light on just how this story began. A few minutes after he is escorted outside and the lights go out. The whispers die down as everyone begins to nod off. The snoring picks up, like the slow and inevitable rising of a tide. Wooden bed frames creak under the weight of pilgrims tossing and turning their way back to sleep. I shove my headphones back in, cramming in the silence. I once more tie a shirt around my oh-so-sensitive face. The rain trickles back on, the thunder calling me to dreamland.

And then I hear shouting.

"Help me! Help me! Somebody help me!"

It's the Dutchman.

The shouting grows intense, his deep voice booming from the room nearby. We all assume the worst — that he is being beaten by the police — and once more the lights flash on. Pilgrims rush out to intervene, others blink away the disorientation and sit up, confused once more by the midnight disarray.

A Frenchman hops down from his bunk and works to rally the uncommitted bystanders to the aid of his fellow *peregrino*.

"Eee is jest a pilgreem! WE are all jest pilgreems! We must 'elp him!'"

His arms are raised as he storms up and down the bunk rows, passionately shouting at us in his thick French accent. A waving Tricolour would hardly seem out of place, the building of a barricade and the storming of the Bastille a natural next step. The doors are yanked open by other pilgrims, and we discover that the Dutchman isn't, in fact, being beaten — he simply doesn't want to be arrested. Nevertheless, the French pilgrim continues to shout his rebellion into the foreign dark of a Spanish night as the police take their man outside. They fold the lumbering Dutchman in half and stuff him into the back of their cruiser. The rallying cry of the Frenchman fades as the blue lights from the police car flash into the distance, throwing shadows along the walls of our crowded *albergue*. It's all over in minutes. No one starts to sing *Les Mis*.

Instead, folks chatter away until they begin to realize it's the middle of the night. One by one, they crawl back into bed, myself included. I'm left to bask in an eerie quiet of my fictitious thunderstorm, to ponder away the few remaining hours of the night from the comfort of my cozy bottom bunk.

Through my whispered conversations (and yes, some eavesdropping) I discover the man perhaps had a wee bit too much of that ever-so-affordable Spanish wine. Having over-consumed the Bacchanalian beverage, he decided the official 10 p.m. curfew of the hostel was more of a "suggestion" then a hard and fast rule. A rather displeased woman thought such anarchy inappropriate and the two had a verbal disagreement. This led to her calling the police, and said police showing up and arresting the Flying Dutchman. The End, I suppose. Chances are the story is more complicated — they often are — but as I drift off it makes me think.

We are not, as the Frenchman declared, *just* pilgrims. None of us here on the Camino de Santiago are just pilgrims. We are not just travellers — we are all far more, for better or for worse. We all have histories and baggage. We are all the sum of a million different thoughts and a million different actions — every day. Hell, every moment. The Dutchman was not just a pilgrim: he was a pilgrim AND a man breaking the curfew AND a man who maybe had too much cheap wine. Though that is, I admit, hardly grounds to arrest anyone.

So yeah, we are all pilgrims. But we are so much more, too.

~~~~~

A few days later, we pass the Flying Dutchmen. It's around lunchtime in a small, dusty town whose name I've long forgotten (and probably never even knew in the first place). In the span of us walking through the shade of a medieval church he downs two beers. By the time I unsling my pack to grab my water bottle he has cracked open and gulped a third, crushing the cans and tossing them in a rusted-out garbage bin. He props himself up in the shade as we pass, though whether he recognizes us I can't tell. I wish him a *Buen Camino* as we stroll by.

Within a sweaty hour he has caught up to us, his muscled legs carrying him at an impressive clip. His skin is tanned, hardened. His eyes are hidden behind slick sunglasses that keep the oppressive glare of a Spanish summer at bay. We make small talk as he passes, tip-toeing around the incident. Polite words exchanged, he nods his farewell and picks up his pace to one well beyond our abilities. As he speeds away across the bright and burning *meseta*, he glances over his shoulder and shouts his final words to us, words I take to heart.

"Don't give in!"

5474

A Lesson in Taking Risks

I'm in a hotel — no, a motel — in Jackson Hole, Wyoming. With me are two strangers I met only recently, strangers who I have spent every waking moment with for the past...I don't even know. The days blur like faded highway lines, like the brown-green smears of forests that have lined the countless highways I've been driving for at least a few thousand miles now. Those days have come and gone like hectic cities, each brimming with an abundance of chaotic life, the details more a *feeling* than a precise memory.

Until now.

I'm eating vegan s'mores in bed, a ridiculous smile forming on my dumb face. I know this will be a memory that sticks, lodged in my ribcage, too monumental to ever shake itself free.

This is an adventure.

The thought coaxes my smile to bloom as I prop myself up against the tacky wallpaper, looking over to my two companions who are cozily sprawled in the twin bed beside me. They drew the short straws, leaving me to enjoy the comfort of an entire bed to myself. When you're road tripping on a budget, an entire bed — hell, any bed — is a luxury worth cherishing.

For the past three odd weeks, I've been touring the US of A

as part of my job. I'm the Community Manager for one of the world's biggest (and best) travel blogs. Part of that job entails traveling the world and organizing events for fellow travellers.

Yeah, that's a real job.

On this cross-country tour of Uncle Sam's backyard, I've met hundreds of like-minded travellers and nomads. I've traded stories until my voice grew hoarse and sore. I've slept on strangers' couches and been given personal tours of their cities. I've been bought meals by people I don't know. I've slept on a boat and set a new record for the fastest I've even been driven in a car (190km/hour — thanks Cole!). I've had a vegan po'boy and learned what a "shotgun apartment" is. I've played soccer with Trump supporters, seen more roadkill then I ever thought possible, and talked to a slang-spewing gang member who called me the n-word on numerous occasions.

I've been running on a handful of hours of sleep each day, fueled by a French co-pilot who keeps me hydrated with tap water, energy drinks, and a hilarious accent. Calling the backseat home is Ellie, a sassy American from Rancho Cucamonga who drops *your mom* jokes like it's 1999. With them, the days of the week are mere phantoms. The future is an illusion, a shimmering highway mirage.

This is an adventure.

This is where routine and boundaries and expectations go to die, buried six feet under carefree chaos and a giving in to the inevitable. I eat s'mores at their funeral and laugh myself to sleep, remembering how this whole impromptu trip got started...

~~~~~

I was the only white person at the bus stop. After riding

public transit a few times around Charlotte, North Carolina I began to realize that, *down here* white folks don't take the bus. *Down here*, most of the white folks have shiny new Escalades or pick-up trucks and actively avoid riding the bus — especially if that bus was a 12-hour jaunt all the way to New Orleans.

For $20, though, I couldn't pass up the deal.

I chatted up a friendly couple as I waited for the budget-friendly Megabus to arrive. They were a doughy, middle-aged pair who were all smiles and chuckles, a charmingly stereotypical embodiment of that southern hospitality. Admittedly, I struggled with their accents. The occasional slang swirled with a southern drawl to form phrases my mind couldn't unravel fast enough in conversation. I did my best to muddle through, politely smiling and nodding wherever I got lost. If anything can give that southern hospitality a run for its money, it's Canadian politeness.

Sporadically interjecting into the conversation was a spry, foul-mouthed (but jovial) man with the words BATH SALTS tattooed across his face. Shoulders bent forward in a perpetual swagger, he couldn't have stood much taller than 5'5" and likely weighed under a buck twenty. Yet whatever physical intimidation was lacking from his physique was unequivocally made up for with his confident attitude — and his grill. His teeth were plated and capped with reflective layers of gold and silver, the metals dazzling in the late-morning sun as he rambled and cursed his way through conversations. The faded scribblings of dated tattoos were etched on every free inch of skin, extending up his neck to cover of his face. He dropped more n-bombs that I had ever heard as he recounted tales of his criminal past, much to the amusement of everyone around. As unconventional as he appeared, he had a knack for weaving a tale and everyone was entertained by his over-exaggerated anecdotes. He ended up sitting near me when the bus to *Nawwlins* finally pulled in, spending his time en route hitting on the curvaceous woman behind him. She was twice his size and packed enough sass to rival his swagger. I confess, it was an amusing back and forth to occasionally eavesdrop in on whenever I got tired of reading or nodding off to an open-mouth nap. He was persistent, I'll give him that.

I listened to him as he prated on and off for the better part of a day, our bus lumbering along the highways and bayous of Louisiana. Pulling into the terminal long after sunset, I hopped off the bus and onto the touristy tram, riding the rails toward the French Quarter. The shape of tents and cardboard lean-tos could be seen lining the shadowy strips under an overpass, a handful of homeless men camped out at the bus stop itself. I hadn't been in the city for five minutes before I encountered a heavily intoxicated man spewing racist remarks into the humid night air. Everyone on the tram seemed to just ignore him as we crawled past, though an uncomfortable flush washed over the passengers. No one replied as the racist raved and ranted, we all just stared at him, confused and transfixed.

My destination was across town, walking distance from the French Quarter. I was to be couch surfing with a local who lived in a shotgun apartment. It was smack dab in the middle of a hipster neighbourhood, and the bars leaked moustachioed patrons out into the night as I passed. Leaving the ironically rowdy bar scene behind me, I wandered up and down some quiet residential streets until I found the address. Upon arrival, I began to realize that the accommodation was…well, it wasn't exactly what I was expecting.

Which, I suppose, is my own fault for having expectations.

The house itself was run down, with a weathered and frayed couch plopped squarely on the front porch. A lanky fellow with a few days' worth of stubble was curled up upon it, half asleep. I figured him to be one of the roommates or someone from the attached apartment. My assumption was incorrect.

Kind soul that my host was, he let a homeless fellow crash on his porch each night, allowing the man some makeshift reprieve from the coastal elements. While I thought this to be a very generous and kind offer, it did make me second guess my choice of accommodation, if only out of some vague concern for my safety. Maybe that was a reasonable concern, or maybe I was just being uppity and close-minded. I don't know. What I do know is that the dude on the couch was not the worst of it. Not by a long shot.

Opening the door to the apartment, I was greeted by a warzone. It made my hotel in Beijing look like the goddamn Ritz. The walls were long-since peeled and every inch of the place was covered in clutter; dusty records, milk crates full of knickknacks, and bed sheets covering the windows were but some of the chaos my eyes took in. The lighting was dim, and dust danced silky trails in the air. It smelled lived in and weary.

It was then, walking deeper into the rectangular abode, that I learned what a shotgun apartment is. A shotgun apartment requires one to walk through each preceding room before you arrive in the next. With a door on each end, you could — in theory — stand at one door and shoot a shotgun clear through the other. Why you would want or need to do that is beyond me. The design, however, meant that everyone had to walk through my room to access the bathroom and kitchen. It is actually a rather neat setup, though one that doesn't accommodate the sort of privacy many of us are used to. But I managed, as there was a small curtain fastened around the bed so I could at least block out some of the light (and prying eyes). It wasn't fancy, but it worked.

The kitchen and bathroom were something else altogether. I don't think either had been cleaned in a decade, with dead bugs and mold found on every exposed surface. The dated smell of decomposing food clung to the walls, and I made a mental note to stick to the restaurants in town. It may have been a ramshackle dump of a crash pad, but it was free and my host was genuine and kind, so who am I to judge? In for a penny, in for a pound.

I chatted with my host's roommate for a while, a friendly and rotund man who I pegged to be in his late 40's. It wasn't until the end of our conversation that I got a glimpse of him, for he was sprawled in his own room, laying in the cool dark next to an open window that trickled in a breeze. He was pale and sweaty, with a loose t-shirt covering his torso. It protruded outward in an odd fashion, so much so that I stole a second glance. It turns out the man wasn't nearly as rotund as I thought — he just had what looked like a giant tumor growing on his body.

While I felt bad for his plight, I also couldn't help but chuckle to myself. *Of course the middle-aged roommate laying half naked in the dark has a giant growth on his body.* I wasn't quite in over my head here, but I was certainly swimming when I expected to be on shore, if you take my meaning.

After a night out at a blues bar, I rolled into my single bed, pinning the curtain closed around me. Staring at the brown spots on the ceiling, I basked in the unexpected chaos of the adventure. I fell asleep wondering just what else the Road would have in store for me.

Turns out, it would be a lot.

The next day I rose early and headed off to a co-working space where I happened to meet Tristan. He was a lanky and baby-faced French traveller, wandering the globe on a year-long, round-the-world trip. Along the way, he was meeting with experts in the clean tech field, having himself working in the tech industry in Central Asia for some time. We chatted a bit and discovered that our itinerary was almost exactly the same. We would both be going to Texas, after which we would then head north to Seattle. I offered him the co-pilot seat in my car, which I was going to pick up in Austin after my next leg. He agreed without much thought, and we parted ways with plans to meet in Texas in a few days.

And meet we did.

I grabbed my rental car and rolled around town to pick Tristan up. We chatted, feeling out the vibe as we cruised toward Dallas. We shared stories of life and love and adventure and all things in between. He was a carefree traveller, something of my opposite. Where I liked to have a loose-fitting plan and make sure I know what is happening, Tristan flew by the seat of his French pantaloons. It was liberating to get to bask in that relaxed state of travelling for a while, to hear stories from his carefree wanderings. Naturally, he had his share of hiccups, but he simply chalked it all up to part of the adventure. His *c'est la vie* attitude was inspiring, and I promised to embrace as much of it as I could.

But first, we had a problem to solve.

You see, a road trip isn't a road trip if you don't name your car. Your car is a part of the adventure — part of the team. It's your home, your sacred craft of exploration. Even during non-road trips, I was a fan of naming the vehicles I was using. Our old family station wagon from when I was a kid was *Betsy*. The van my best friend drove us to university in was *Slave 1*. My Icelandic road trip was made possible by our little beast of a car, *Lava*.

And so now it was time to ponder a name for our car, something fitting for the road ahead. Naturally, we would need a few days to see how it ran, to see what quirks it manifested, how it rolled with the punches of adventure.

So we waited.

~~~~~

A few days later we found ourselves in Denver, at a sports bar, of all places. It was packed, brimming with rowdy patrons decked out in matching jerseys. It was a jovial sea of red, with novelty hats and painted faces stoking the boisterous social fire. While I've always enjoyed playing sports I never was one to go wild on the fandom. These folks, though? They drank that shit up. I don't even know what sport was on TV, let alone what team. Fortunately for me, I wasn't there for the match.

I was hosting a travel meetup in town and the bar seemed a good fit. Our rag-tag group of about 25 backpackers took over the patio, jostling for space near one of the outdoor fire pits that kept the late-summer chill at bay. I did the rounds, chatting up everyone and encouraging them all the mingle, to meet new people. That was the point of this, after all: to bring travellers together.

That's when I met Ellie.

A short, sassy red-head from California, Ellie walked an amusing line between confident and awkward. She just happened to be visiting a friend in Denver and decided to come hang out before her flight home to L.A, which was in a few hours. Tristan, the devilish vagabond that he is, had something else in mind.

"You should come with us! Chris will be going to California...eventually. He can take you!"

By the time Tristan ushered me over for a casual introduction the deal had already been sealed.

"This is Ellie. She is coming with us."

I didn't bat an eye. This was an adventure, after all, and I had promised myself I would be more spontaneous. I welcomed her with open arms.

"The more the merrier!"

And boy were we merry.

Over the next few days we saw buffalo in Yellowstone, hiked around the snow-dusted peaks of Grand Teton National Park, and took more jump photos than I ever thought possible in the process. Ellie and I even learned a few French lyrics from some French songs, allowing us to mumble through the chorus when we felt like having a sing along.

And we even — after much debate — came up with a fitting name for our car. We hummed and hawed, deliberating over each suggestion until the universe provided us the perfect answer: The J-Hole.

Named in honour of Jackson Hole, Wyoming (which was named after God knows what), it felt right immediately, like the Hand of Fate itself had guided us to where we needed to be. It was weird, it was unique, and it was kind of gross. It was a perfect fit. Naturally, that made us the J-Hole Crew.

But as with all adventures, it wasn't all sunshine and Oreos.

After an unusual two nights at a Couchsurfing host with OCD and a dog that liked to bite, we rolled out toward Idaho with Ellie now calling the backseat home.[37] Oreos, energy drinks, and baguettes fueled the journey as we made our way northwest, strangers slowly but surely fusing into friends. Being budget backpackers, we opted to avoid unnecessary expenses as often as we could along the way. Sometimes, those "unnecessary expenses" were beds.

As we drove into the darkening night of autumn in Idaho, we decided that legitimate accommodation was not needed: we would get all cozy in the J-Hole and save ourselves a few bucks in the process. Seemed like a good idea at the time.

It wasn't.

Without any blankets, we rummaged through the trunk for anything that might suit our needs. We grabbed our towels and extra sweaters to bundle up, parking ourselves in a gravel lot between potholes at a run-down truck stop. In the trunk was a bag of miscellaneous crap from my boss, a garbage bag of stuff I was supposed to drop off at the Salvation Army a few thousand miles ago. Fortunately, I didn't.

And it made all the difference.

In the bag were a set of old curtains which we used to insulate our temporary shelter. We draped the curtains over each window, keeping the drafty night air at bay. For a while, anyway.

I cranked the heat as we drifted to sleep, hoping our bodies would warm the car and keep us from freezing the death. Lamentably, our budget-savvy brains forget to factor in one minor detail when it came to our camp out: the altitude.

We were a few thousand feet above sea level at this point, and it was decidedly not warm. I shivered myself to sleep in short bursts, never managing more than an uncomfortable thirty minutes at a time. By 3 a.m., there were thin tendrils of ice forming on the windshield. Like spider webs, they stretched out slowly, patiently, until they enveloped their prey in a shivering chill. That's when I made the call.

I slid my hand from under my towel, the air frosty to the touch. I turned on the car, desperately blasting the heat. Smiling to myself in the darkness, I huddled against dash as my skin regained feeling. I did this every thirty minutes for the remaining hours of the night. When the dawn lazily wrestled itself onto the horizon, I grabbed a handful of Oreos, thumbed open a Red Bull, and carried on down the highway, concluding that a bed sometimes *is* a necessary expense.

None of us had a particularly enjoyable rest that night, though that didn't stop us from trying it again a few weeks later in California. Tristan, who was set to depart in Seattle, carried on with us down the Pacific Coast Highway, prodding us to once more forego comfort and embrace adventure. His ridiculous and charming accent was too hard to say no to. Once more, we gave up our creature comforts for the sake of our budget.

Again, not a great idea.

Another night was spent shivering in a questionable location, this time along some winding back road in a valley just off the interstate. Well off the beaten path, it was quiet and remote, the sort of place someone might go to hide a body. It seemed like one of the few places in all of California where no artificial light could be seen, and we didn't see or hear anyone for the entirety of the night. I wasn't sure if that was comforting or concerning.

But we could see the stars, and as I huddled myself to sleep with a towel draped over my shoulders for warmth, I figured even this — a terrible sleep in a cramped, dirty rental car — wasn't so bad after all.

~~~~~

The final leg of our trip came when we arrived in L.A. Without question, this was my least favorite place to drive in all of the country. San Francisco was bad, but the congestion in L.A was beyond sluggish. Walking was no doubt faster. And the public transportation? You have to smell it to believe it. But it was here, in the City of Flowers and Sunshine, that we met the final member of our J-Hole crew.

Angela was a fashion student with a cozy flat way over in

Hollywood. She was friendly, if a bit shy, with bombshell blonde looks. Tristan, the charming Frenchman that he is, chatted her up and once more sung that siren song of Adventure. By the end of the night, Angela was in the car with us and we were off to meet our ending. We had decided if we were going out, we were going out with a bang.

So, we drove to Vegas.

Katy Perry blared as we pumped ourselves up for our yolo curtain call. I had been on the road for almost 2 months now, and I felt it was time to splurge. I booked us in for a luxurious two nights in the Monte Carlo. It seemed a fitting way to end our fellowship. And after travelling almost 20,000 kilometres by plane, train, bus, and car, I deserved a queen size bed. Or, at least half of one.

And so came the ending.

Over the next couple days we wandered and laughed and gambled and drank. We ripped out to the Grand Canyon to watch a storm blow in, scrambling along its precarious curves to capture the remaining days of our travels together. We had photoshoots and pillow fights. We fought that final night with every ounce of our being until exhaustion had us drifting off to sleep, the flame of our adventure blown out.

That was the end of the J-Hole Crew, in all her chaos, all her glory.

~~~~~

For the first time in weeks I am alone, powering the J-Hole through the sparse and arid landscapes of Nevada. I pass the time on the empty highway counting road kill. 51 deer. 3 coyotes. A handful of rabbits. More birds than I can remember. Maybe a dog, I'm not sure. The battered corpses guide me home, piecemeal witnesses to the conclusion of my adventure. Dashboard Confessional blares through the scratchy speakers, washing waves of emo acoustic guitar over me. I belt out lyrics to keep the silence at bay, choking on my tightening throat as I fight back tears.

Goodbyes are never easy.

It isn't until I'm somewhere out in the desert beyond the glitzy glow of Vegas that I remember I was supposed to check to see how many miles we drove together. Glancing down at the odometer, I do some mental math and make a note.

5,474 miles. We drove five-thousand four-hundred and seventy-four miles together. Almost 9,000 kilometres.

I run through the trip in my mind, etching as much of it into stone as I can. It's a furious blur. Every mile, an adventure. Every adventure, a memory, embedded deep. The number serves as a reminder to take risks, to reach out, to give in. To accept the chaos of the Road in all its bitter glory.

5,474. The numbers are now inked on my skin, a perpetual reminder that adventure, more than anything, is a state of mind. It's there, always calling, a siren song well worth the trouble.

Do you hear it?

But more importantly, will you answer?

Christopher Kevin Oldfield

Moonwalking Murle and the Bastard Boys of I-COY

A Lesson in *Home*

"OLDFIELD!"

My eyes darted up, searching. It was the booming voice of my Warrant Office, and I scanned the scene to find him. His tall and lean figure stood a full head above the rest of us, his hand just completing a tap of his beret as my eyes found him. It was the signal for me to haul ass. I was already in motion.

I hustled across the tent-lined square, kicking up dust as the gravel crunched under my shoddy and unattractive running shoes. They were plain and grey, chosen to match my plain and grey socks, my plain and grey cotton shorts, and my plain — but white — t-shirt. The pièce de résistance was my floppy, tan Tilly hat, complete with fetching chin strap and 360-degree brim.

Welcome, my friends, to the military.

...or, rather, the cadet corps.

(The "p" is silent.)

I was 14, and it was my first time away from home beyond sleepovers and visiting relatives. For two weeks, I marched and drilled and yelled at other kids as we stomped our way around the parade square. I slept on a military cot in a musty tent with 11 other kids from Ontario, Canada. I learned important skills, like how to clean a rifle and how to hide in the bush — vital skills every 14-year-old needs.

I have a handful of memories from those two weeks, all of which I look back on with a fond and brimming nostalgia. Within my first few days at Blackdown — the cadet training center where we were located — I was put not only in charge of my tent, but my entire platoon. A few days later and I was overseeing the company drill team as well. I worked hard. I followed orders. I loved every minute of it.

And I loved the other cadets who made up my platoon, from the scrappy Private Burger to the chubby Private Sergeant to the only kid who wasn't Caucasian in our entire platoon, Private Murle. Under the predatory gaze of our Warrant Office, Murle was a saint — we all were — but when free to his own devices he would incorporate a moonwalk into as much military drill as was humanly possible. His gleaming boots would catch the sun as they slid across the parade square, his face beaming with a smug grin that betrayed the fact that he knew just how cool he was. I let him get away with it as often as I could, simply because I could. We were kids, and it was our small rebellion, our inside joke when the adults weren't around.

As smile-inducing as the memory of moonwalking Murle is, the memory that I find most is my first phone call home. While I had only been away one week, and while I was only a handful of hours from home, a phone call was nevertheless obligatory. I can see the scene in my mind as clearly as I saw it that day, a vivid postcard from a bygone age.

~~~~~

Christ it's hot.

In the thirty-something degree heat, I strolled over to the

payphone and waited in line for my turn, lungs already huffing. The sticky heat was blanketing my skin like a wet, heavy rag. I lined up in the shade of the overhanging roof, the elongated grey building a drab edition to the stark surrounds. The white concrete was newly poured and recently swept. The uninspired palate matched our military-issue clothing, the only colour I remember coming from the sharp blue sky, freshly painted and flecked with white, fluffy pucks.

The metal exterior of the phone booth was scorching hot, so much so that the cadets would lean against the coarse bricks or half squat to avoid touching it. They hid in the shade as they talked and waited, desperate to keep themselves out of the worst of the clawing, weighty heat. Dust and sweat tickled our lips and throat incessantly, leave sporadic coughs and spits to poke through the murmured conversations. I took a swig from my canteen, passing it up the line as I waited for quarters to expire, fanning my face with my Tilly.

I wasted no time when my turn came. I thumbed a single quarter into the slot — because payphones used to only cost a quarter — and dialed home.[38] And then I felt it. My heart started to beat a little faster, my throat slowly tightened. As the phone rang, my jaw tensed.

I was on the brink of crying.

I had no real idea why. I was truly loving my time, I was safe and sound, and, geographically speaking, I was not even that far from home. Yet, as soon as my mom answered the call I was fighting hard not to burst into tears in front of the other cadets. We had just spent an hour marching two steps forward, one step back under the sweltering gaze of a late-summer sun as punishment for a minor infraction I have long forgotten. During that march, sweat poured off me like I was an open faucet, sizzling onto asphalt that was hot enough to cook an egg...and I didn't bat an eye as I called out the repetitive orders. Yet somehow simply saying hello to my mom led my voice to crack and strain? Don't get me wrong, I love my family but even I was surprised. What was it that choked me up? What is it about being away from home that can bring us to tears?

Nowadays — seventeen years or so later — I'm used to being away. I've learned to accept that "staying home" is an impossibility for me. At least for now. For those of us who live or work abroad or who travel often enough to be considered nomadic, home is something of a tricky subject. For us, home can be a tough nut to crack. Is home where your mailing address is? Is it where your friends and family are? Where you grew up? Is it where the majority of your possessions are, that place where your books or DVDs or maybe even a rarely-used suit is kept? Maybe home is just the run-down hostel you're presently crashing in, a creaky bunk in a room full of odorous — but lovely — backpackers. Maybe home is a 12-man tent that you share with a bunch of other kids trying to figure out who they are as they polish boots and march drill.

I used to think that, the more I wander about, the more home would lose its meaning. But now, as I've chewed on thoughts of home, I think it's perhaps the opposite.

These days, I have an apartment in Sweden. I can mumble enough of the language to get by, allowing me to navigate the country without too much embarrassment. I pay rent, I pay (a lot) of taxes, I shop at Swedish grocery stores. It's home, and day by day it grows more familiar.

And that, I think, is partly what home is: a familiar space.

Which is why "home" keeps expanding its meaning to me. The more I travel around, the more familiar I am with the world at large — and with myself. Home isn't just small-town Canada anymore, it's now Sweden *and* Canada. But it's more than that, too. I've been to a lot of different places over the past thirty years but even I'm not familiar with every nook and cranny of the wild blue yonder. However, I am familiar with being lost. With exploring. With gruesome shock and unexpected heartbreak. With researching new cities. With sleeping on floors and cots and couches, in hostels and hotels and airports and military-issue tents. I'm familiar with meeting new people, at home and abroad, and sharing my life with them. I'm familiar with the act of opening up and letting go.

After thirty-plus years and over forty-plus countries, I'm comfortable in my own skin, regardless of the imaginary borders and waving flags that surround me. I've come to accept that my roots are not in any one place, but connected to the people I've come to know and love. My roots are limitless, unbound by any distance. They are connected to the moment, wherever I may be.

When I call home now — using Facetime instead of a beat-up payphone — there is no welling of tears nor building of tension in my throat. That doesn't mean I don't love my family or that I don't miss them, because I do. But home is where your heart is, and my heart is splayed upon a map.

Christopher Kevin Oldfield

Saying Goodbye at the End of the World

A Lesson in Endings

It's the end of the world.

I look out to the horizon and see nothing but the ocean, grey and flat. Sparse and lazy curves bob and roll along its extend surface, adding texture to the panorama. I stare, a mix of emotions too raw to decipher sitting heavy in my gut. I hold my view, eyes glazing to the subtlety of change. The waves mimic one another as I follow them toward the shore. They come and go, capping white before breaking themselves against the rocks below. A part of me wants to pity their fate, their ceaseless onslaught. But I know each and every wave is making a difference. In 10,000 years, these rocks will be sand. Persistence, I've learned, is everything.

For as far as I can see, the waves extend forever. An infinite and inevitable ending. Sitting there, against the jagged stones of Cape Finisterre, I feel small and alone. The rocky peninsula was once thought to be the physical end of the world, a place the Romans considered to be the last bastion of land before eternal emptiness. It is here where I am about to say goodbye to a dear friend. Together we have marched almost 800km along the Camino de Santiago, only to arrive at an inescapable farewell.

An ending.

We had met, quite coincidently, in France. I had just crossed the Pyrenees on foot, an act that was far more challenging than I had anticipated...though admittedly, my physical preparation was a far cry from admirable. With virtually no training, I departed the sleepy town of Saint Jean Pied de Port at dawn and headed into the hills. Ahead of me was a 29km hike, one I managed more out of stubbornness than any sort of physical prowess. The continual ups and downs were taxing, a constant grind on my weakening knees. The trek required a perpetual *leaning in* as the unstoppable winds that battered the mountainside pushed back against my meagre efforts forward. The cutting shriek of banshee gales drowned out all other noise, leaving me to reflect on the stunning vistas that knelt before the summit. It was August, and it was hot.

With a sweat-soaked back I worked my way ever closer to the Spanish border, my joints taking the brunt of the burden as I sidestepped down the mountainside. I had left the paved roads behind, having entered the forests and fields that forever painted the landscape. Wherever there wasn't the greens and browns of grass and trees there were the azure streaks of a bright summer sky. Gentle wisps of clouds were the only blemishes on the canvas above, white flecks that disappeared hastily under the windy charge of the mountain range.

It was there, in the borderlands of France, that we met. Tromping down a narrow switchback, I saw him out of the corner of my eye. He was alone, separated from the pilgrim crowds as he rested in the shade on the woodland floor. He was a rather big fellow, thick and stout and faded by the elements. It wasn't long past sunrise, the day still brand new, yet he looked worn, tired. He had, I gathered, been sitting there a while. At first glance, he looked a little rough around the edges and I was tempted to just keep going...but something compelled me. Stepping off the trail, I reached out and extended my arm in friendship.

I helped him up off the ground, and within moments we had bonded. For the next 30 days, he and I were inseparable. We became the best of friends, helping each other through all the Camino had to offer: sharp wind and icy rain, heavy fog and scorching heat. We were a team, he and I, and I honestly doubt I would have managed the journey without him.

But every journey has an end. Ours took place, quite fittingly, at *finis terrae*. The End of the World.

My companion had never seen the ocean, so we sat on the rocks and listened to the waves together, lost in their fated symphony. Blanketed in a thick mist, we sat there as the minutes bled, other pilgrims coming and going. We clung to that last act, refusing to embrace the curtain call that awaited us. We had worked so hard to get here, yet now that we had reached our goal we were lost: there was nothing left to chase.

And so the ending came.

With a final silent embrace and a kiss for luck, I said goodbye to my companion and turned around, taking my first steps toward home in over a month. My jaw was awkwardly tense as I stifled a tear, not wanting to be seen sobbing as I weaved between the gathered pilgrims.

Don't cry, don't cry, don't cry.

Leaving the waves to their well-earned finale, I left the coastline. When I last looked back, I saw that he was leaning against a red and rusted metal tower, watching me disappear into the crowds and fog of the world's end.

His name was Jefferson Smalls and I would never see him again. He was my walking stick.

Christopher Kevin Oldfield

can we live here for a second?
hold the line of this moment so we can know, truly
be the mass of it and bear it onward
bare it, onward
for another chance at another rest
where we can simmer in its holding
let it rustle us
and send us tumbling on
caressing the cobbled and roughshod parts we've
orchestrated.
it's a beautiful tune

Christopher Kevin Oldfield

Explosions and Rare Moments

A Lesson in Conclusions and Clarity

On a night bus in Cambodia I sat awake, sleepless and cramped. From my bunk-bed seat I watched the rain splatter and roll against the glass. We sped along a dimly-lit dirt road at breakneck speeds that left me wishing for an extra seat belt. I was sitting up in the semi-darkness, propped against a folded sweater as I listened to music. The ethereal scenery was a kaleidoscope blur, forcing me to squint through the smeared droplets of rain into the hazy shadows of the Khmer Kingdom. My iPod fed melodic sounds directly into my brain, lulling me serene as I bounced in my seat. My size thirteen shoes were jammed awkwardly in the undersized seat-bed, tingling as I shifted every few moments to stay comfortable. With each inhalation, I choked down a very human concoction of sweat and feet and stale breath, a familiar odour I had grown indifferent to after a few months on the road. There were, I had come to realize, far worse smells one encounters in South East Asia.

I had been on the continent for over four months, with no immediate plans to head home. While I could describe how I got there — the flights and trains and buses that led me from home — it took me some time to understand why I was there, some 13,000 kilometres from home.

I had completed university with a bachelor's in history, spending the subsequent years chasing lacklustre paychecks to no worthwhile avail. It was then when I found the edges of my life growing dull; I was having trouble finding my spark. The embers of passion that once fueled me seemed to have slipped from my grasp, the effects of which were trickling into my life. Excitement, curiosity, purpose — they were all fading into an indifferent acceptance of an uninteresting life. Finally, I felt it was time to change, to let go; my appetite was no longer satiated by simply carrying on. I was being smothered by the mundane mechanics of a regular life and I needed some air. I needed to shake things up, to draw closer to the marrow of what it meant to be to be *me*. I needed to break out, to shed my skin and look at the world with my own eyes, to look at myself with my own eyes. I needed to reconnect, with myself and the world. Our stories were intertwined, yet the world at large felt so unfamiliar. Distant, unfocused, and forever out of reach. I suppose a part of me was in search of the unsearchable, those moments only found when you least expect them: when you are buried in the present, swept away by the current of *being*. Those moments are electric. They serve as emotional kindling, keeping the fires in us burning; they keep the night at bay.

13,000 kilometres from home, I was searching for my fire.

That search brought me to Asia, where I found myself perpetually perched upon the fence between serenity and chaos, sporadically dipping my toes into the nourishing cosmic waters of each. This journey of mine had brought me to poverty-stricken Cambodia, a nation shrouded in the bloody remnants of a violent history. It was there where unlucky families slept outdoors on sagging slabs of cardboard, where children were well schooled in the art of hustling change from privileged tourists and grimy (but also privileged) backpackers — all to the harassing tune of "Tuk-Tuk?" echoing in the chaotic cityscape.

I was a world away from home, engulfed in a foreign culture that I would only ever catch the merest glimpse of. It was there, drifting recklessly through the breathless night, that it hit me.

Clarity, like a breath of cold, sharp air, filled me. The world fell into focus, and for the first time in since my monastery days, everything made sense. Time felt crisp and sharp and tangible. I felt connected, unfiltered. For the first time in a long time, I felt like *me*. I could feel the music now, my headphones spilling sonic hurricanes deep into my veins. Every bump in the road was like a cascading wave washing over me, anchoring me home. In every droplet of clear rain upon the dirty glass I could see the life and death of all of us. The tired stench of weary feet became the sacred perfume of adventure. I couldn't help but smile — to myself, to the darkness, to everything that brought me to that moment. I was consumed, burned away completely as the bus bounced along the half-paved road into the familiar pitch of an unknown land. I was reborn in a perfect moment. I was afire.

~ ~ ~ ~ ~

Those moments, the moments that fuel us, are hard to come by. They are magical and elusive, yet profound in their simplicity and their ability to open us up to the world. When our blinders come off, when the layers are peeled away and we truly connect with the moment — that is always a transformative experience. It may not make for captivating story telling. It may not sell books nor demonstrate your epic travel skills, but it *will* demonstrate your quality as a genuine human being. Which is good enough for me.

More than any adventure, it is those moments I hold dear. They are what sustain me, at home and abroad. They are vast glimpses beyond ourselves, both stark and necessary. And just like life on the road, you never really know what you will see. And you don't need to travel half-way across the world to dive into those moments, either. To find your kindling, your fire. They are there, with you, no matter where you roam.

Travel is merely a tool, a way to shock us into remembering the moment. It's a reminder that we are all connected, that there really is no escape from *right now* — from *you* — regardless of how far away you fly from home.

~~~~~

Years later, I still play that same album I listened to on that bus in Cambodia. I submerge myself in the calm acceptance that arises. Within the first few bars of music, I am both transformed and transported, held steadfast to the moment yet simultaneously catapulted back to Asia. I am dragged through the chaotic mess of markets and sprawl and poverty that is Cambodia. I recall both the kindness I was shown as well as the violence that forged its modern history. Those flashes of Cambodia soon bleed into blue-sky road trips and automatic seat belts, bulbous blisters and creaking bunk beds. In the rushing tide of strobe-light nostalgia I can see the dogs of nam before me, alive and well. We swirl together, a bastard mix of calm and chaos. With every note, every memory, I am once more blindsided by the overwhelmingness of being alive. I am reborn, unencumbered. I am lost. I am home.

seek home
the seldom held aloft
pillars mark us
stark, but landed;
we are greater things

Endnotes

[1] Magical for those privileged enough to visit. Disney is no doubt significantly less magical for the kids in sweatshops making all that merch we buy, or for the underpaid and overworked employees sweltering in ridiculous, oversized costumes all day.

[2] My forest DID have a lot more porno than theirs, though. I once found a tree fort in the forest near my house which had a secret compartment containing pornographic magazines. Score!

[3] Thanks, Wikipedia.

[4] Ok, the smog lost its charm pretty quickly. My lungs weren't too keen on that.

[5] The "village" was more a spattering of nomadic huts in the vicinity of one another. And by vicinity, I mean they were all a few kilometres from one another. I suppose that counts for neighbours in the steppe.

[6] Are camel dumplings a thing??

[7] The shirt was actually a traditional Japanese robe known as a *samugi* or *samue*. Fashionable.

[8] Apparently, many years ago some children were playing in the forest during toilet dumping and one of the poor little dudes fell into the shitty pit. He was rescued without any serious injury...but man, I bet his parents weren't happy.

[9] The engine was at the back of the bus. I don't know why, so just accept it.

[10] The sound totally reminds me of the bunker alarm from LOST. Talk about flashbacks.

[11] I reported this immediately to the police, with my girlfriend as a witness (she was there, too). They did absolutely nothing.

[12] As part of a bachelor party, we went to a shooting range where each of us could pick two guns and a target. I snagged a Tommy gun as well as a Desert Eagle, two firearms far too unwieldy for a lightweight like myself. One of the other guys paid extra for a grenade launcher. Seriously. For targets, the options were a standard bull's eye (boring), Osama bin Laden

(offensive?), or a zombie. I stand by my choice of zombie. I also played a handful of Texas Hold'em tournaments, and I actually didn't do too badly and won enough money to cover my costs for that trip. I owe those victories to my dearest mother, who taught me how to play poker. Thanks, ma!

[13] We're talking heat in the 105-115F zone, for all you Fahrenheit-using weirdos. 45 Celsius for the normal folks.

[14] Jurassic Park is one of the greatest films ever made. Period. Anyone who disagrees is a terrorist.

[15] It reminded me of that scene in Jurassic Park when they first see the brachiosaurus and Dr. Grant rips off his glasses. *That* epic. Also, I just learned how to spell brachiosaurus.

[16] "SHE DOESN'T EVEN GO HERE!"

[17] That's Celsius, folks. In the inferior Fahrenheit system we're talking around 95-100. Balls hot.

[18] She actually ended up with blisters on her blisters that were on her blisters. These we aptly named INCEPTION blisters.

[19] Ice cream totally falls into the deliciously broad realm of candy. Deal with it.

[20] *Gaijin* is the word for foreigner in Japan, though it's generally considered to be a rather politically incorrect term these days. Of course, that didn't stop people from calling me it.

[21] Hahahahaha Boren!

[22] Red Son was the Soviet version of Superman from a comic series that examined the question: *What if Superman landed in Russia instead of America?* Instead of Superman, he was called Red Son. Three cheers for the Comrade of Steel!

[23] Actual chainsaw. Not a euphemism. Sorry, ladies.

[24] I suppose if you're actually in space then that's cool, too.

[25] Apparently, in Sweden they hold their thumbs instead of crossing their fingers. Whatever.

[26] I once lived with 4 other guys, need I say more?

[27] A few months later I noticed she unfriended me and my Austrian co-pilot on Facebook. Can't win 'em all, I suppose.

[28] For the record, the items in question aren't illegal or ethically suspect in and of themselves. Think fancy digital

equipment or rare antiques and not mountains of heroin or exotic animals.

[29] Or "thongs" as they say Down Under. Weirdos.

[30] It is said that when Julius Caesar made that momentous decision to cross the Rubicon in 49 BC he uttered the phrase *"Let the die be cast."* Having begun an invasion of his own country, the wheels were now in motion; the outcome was now in the hands of Fate.

[31] Living at a monastery likely takes the cake for the hardest thing I've ever done. It was an ongoing psychological and physical warzone, with 6, 10,15, hours of meditation per day. There was even one week where I didn't lay down at all — I sat up every night, tied to a pillar so I would stay upright and awake. It was intense. And Kilimanjaro — specifically, summit day — is a close second place. That's how challenging it is…at least to someone with no preparation.

[32] I mean, obviously there was another choice — quit and go down to my cozy tent — but I paid a couple grand for this trip so you bet your britches I'm getting my money's worth.

[33] I later discovered there are some outfitters who pay better wages and thus remove the pressure from tipping, but this was not one of those outfitters. If you are going to Kili, make sure you work with a reputable company that pays their workers a fair and livable wage.

[34] During both winters I spent in Japan, and during the winter weeks I spent on retreat in Seattle, monks got frostbite. I managed to get away with mere chilblains — swollen, stiff, and cracked hands.

[35] Japanese word for a Zen master.

[36] Known as *katsu*, these shouts/growls are used in the Rinzai lineage to focus oneself and demonstrate oneness.

[37] Long story short, I was my CS host's first guest. To celebrate, I even bought him a guestbook so he would have something future guests could sign. He was a tidy, organized professional with minor social anxiety and was an obvious obsessive compulsive. But I rolled with it. Nobody's perfect, after all! His dog was just as fidgety as he was, and was known

to bite here and there (I had to dodge a few nips during my stay). His apartment was incredible, though, I'll give him that. The view looked out over the entire city. Gorgeous. On my second night there, he hosted another surfer — which is a lot to do for your first time hosting. I found out later that he kicked her out and deleted his account because he found the whole thing too taxing on his OCD. Lesson learned? I don't know. But the bed I had was comfy...so whatever!

[38] Not only did payphones used to cost a quarter, but they used to actually exist. Whacky.

(if my plane goes down
and I taste the end,
please tell the world
I loved her)

About the Author

Vegan, straight-edge, Buddhist, and balding, Chris (that's me!) spends the majority of his time wandering the world in search of adventure and vegan snacks. When not on the road he can be found doing such boring things as reading, writing, losing at chess, and nagging his partner about her dirty dishes. Born and raised in Ontario, Canada, he now lives in Sweden with his partner Christine. He blogs about ethical travel and budget adventures at lessonslearnedabroad.com and is the charming Community Manager for Nomadic Matt at forums.nomadicmatt.com.

Made in the USA
Coppell, TX
16 May 2020